It All Begins With HOPE

Patients, Caregivers & the Bereaved Speak Out

by Ronna Fay Jevne, Ph.D.

San Diego, California

LuraMedia ™

© Copyright 1991 LuraMedia
San Diego, California
International Copyright Secured
Publisher's Catalog Number LM-628
Printed and Bound in the United States of America
Printed on recycled paper.

Photography by Joe Morrissey and Joseph J. Rizzuto
Cover and book design by Carol Jeanotilla, Denver, Colorado

LuraMedia, Inc.
7060 Miramar Road, Suite 104
San Diego, CA 92121

Library of Congress Cataloging-in-Publication Data
Jevne, Ronna Fay.
    It all begins with hope : patients, caregivers, and the bereaved speak out / by
Ronna Fay Jevne.
        p. cm.
    Includes bibliographical references (p.   ).
    ISBN 0-931055-83-0
    1. Sick—Psychology.   2. Hope.   I. Title.
R726.5.J48   1991   90-27159
610'.1'9—dc20   CIP

The author gratefully acknowledges permission from the following publishers for quotations from their copyrighted material:

For the Norman Cousins quotations: From *Head First: The Biology of Hope*. Reprinted by permission of the publisher, E.P. Dutton, New York.

For the Albert Einstein quotations: From *Einstein: A Portrait*. Reprinted by permission of The Hebrew University of Jerusalem, Israel.

For the Ronna Jevne excerpt: Reprinted, by permission of the publishers. "I Have a Dream: A Vision for Psychosocial Care of the Cancer Patient," *Humane Medicine*, Vol. 3, No. 2, November 1987.

For the David Suzuki quotation: From *The Edmonton Journal*, August 26, 1990. Reprinted by permission.

Acknowledgments

To each and every person who boldly shared their experiences in order that this book might happen, my heartfelt thanks. I also gratefully acknowledge the financial contribution of the Donna Cipin Memorial Fund. To Daria Petch, Bob Philp, Vicki Ross, Judy Maynes, Gloria Jones, Rhoda Montgomery, and Judy Cerran, my thanks for your assistance in the preparation of the manuscript. For their supportive editorial style, my thanks to Ruth Butler and Marcia Broucek. A special thanks to my husband, Allen, whose very nature is a wellspring of hope.

This book is dedicated to Dr. Jon Van Heerdan of the Mayo Clinic, Rochester, Minnesota, United States, and to Dr. Mouktar Haidar of Wetaskiwin, Alberta, Canada, each in their own way, exemplars of excellence in medicine and caring. Thank you for your gift of hope.

CONTENTS

I. Experiences of Hope

II. Reflections on Hope

I.

Experiences of Hope

Intrigued by Hope

I am different because of the people in this book. I met them all in a cancer hospital. They, and others equally as unique, touched my life in a way that continues to please and to puzzle me. My ideas about psychology have changed. My ideas about God have changed. My ideas about what is important have deepened. I said years later, "I came here a novice. I left a veteran. The patients and their families were my mentors, autocratic physicians my test, and reverence for life my reward."

There were many little lessons but none so clear as, "There is no right way." Simply that. There is no right way to live, no right way to die, no right way to grieve. There is only the way we are at any given moment. Judgment is wasted energy. We are a function of all the influences, experiences, and persons who have touched our lives. Your answer cannot be mine. We may share understandings, but ultimately I must live my life and you yours.

To understand how and why you live your life the way that you do, I must know something of you...as much of your story as you will share. The more I know you, the more opportunity I have to respect you and to guard against violating that which you value.

In my years of work with cancer patients I have been struck not with the change in mortality statistics (albeit important in some kinds of cancer), but by the stream of individuals who grasped a glimmer of hope and hung on. Few hang on unwaveringly, but many, nevertheless, cling tenaciously to hope, frequently despite contrary messages from pessimistic physicians, family, or community. As one patient put it, "Hope is the art of living."

I did not set out to work with life-threatening illness, although it occurred to me as early as fourteen. I helped care for Freeman, who farmed only a mile away, directed the choir, and always treated me like a daughter. He died of nephritis at the age of forty-six. He was not a model of wisdom. He had regrets and frustrations. Somehow, though, those nine weeks from his diagnosis to his death were to influence the rest of my life.

I recall vividly the warm May day in 1964 when I walked to the mailbox, promising God I would help people when I grew up if God would just give us back Freeman, even for a few days. On my return, Mom announced that Freeman had decided to come home to die. He was being taken off dialysis and would be home that afternoon. I have often wondered if I was unknowingly held to the contract.

Little did I know I was to be privileged to be a constant observer to pain and suffering that for the most part goes unnoticed in our everyday lives.

Science has no categories for suffering and hope. It has no language for meaning. Within the world of biomedical science, practitioners are taught to shun conclusions based on single experiences. Evidence based only on large numbers of cases is to be heeded. The approach is statistical; the exceptions are to be ignored. The difficulty with this view is, as Norman Cousins states in *Head First: The Biology of Hope*, "Statistics obscure souls." Einstein punctuates the dilemma when he says, "It is only to an individual that a soul is given." If someone is ill, they are interested not in the many who die, but in those who survive.

It is not only survival, but the pursuit of life that leaves an impression on me. When people have asked me, "Why do you work in that death house?" my efforts to describe the inspirational component have gone something like this: To the outsider I'm sure it's disconcerting to see the wasting that cancer is so capable of illustrating, but you don't see the courage, the hope. You don't see a young mom fulfill her promise to her young son that she will live to take him to his first day of school. You don't see the joy on the face of the staff when Sam came back from his fishing trip with smoked salmon for all. His pain was out of control, but he didn't care. He wanted to leave all of us with a gift, and he had gone and caught it! You don't see the sincerity on the face of a seven-year-old who paged me to ask if he should tell his two younger sisters that their mom might die today. He was worried that it would be too hard on his dad. You don't see the dedication and vision of an incredible team doing an impossible task. I can think of very few people who in their work have the privilege of seeing courage every day. Each day I was a guest in the most private of dramas — the fight between life and death, with no guarantees. These are some of the stories to which I have been privy.

Each person who speaks in this book is unique, yet each might live just down the street from you. They are not remarkable people. If they are, they have paid for their remarkableness with pain and suffering, thought and reflection. They are, like all of us, in some stage of becoming remarkable. They all, often bluntly, share their experience. Each person has their own language of hurt, their own language of triumph. These are their words.

The telling of a story is always a process of selection. Each person has chosen those experiences of the present and the past that are important to them. I have chosen yet again from those experiences those that I felt somehow captured some aspect of their uniqueness and some component of the universal. The choosing was done without scientific method. I listened to people's stories as much as possible without having a question to which I was seeking an answer. I simply wanted to know, "What has been your experience in the world of illness?"

Theoretically, to be believable the characters in a story must come from somewhere, be somewhere, and be known by someone there. Every story supposedly has a beginning, a middle, and an end. Yet, in the world of illness I saw seemingly common characters do unlikely things in improbable circumstances with unpredictable outcomes. If the stories were made into soap operas, the viewers would say the scripts were overwritten, that things don't really happen that way. And yet they do.

Russel remains disease free. Stan begets courage as he continues his struggle. Dennis is raising his two children. Reuben once again has laughter. Alice has moved on to provide leadership as a director of nursing. Graeme is completing his doctoral studies in the area of grief work. The stories did not start when I met these people or end when our paths separated. We journeyed only one brief chapter together.

In a world of disconcerting circumstances the one remarkable display of hope is the profoundness and resilience of the human spirit. This . . . in the presence of no apparent justice. There is no immunity. There is just the courage of the silent hero and the support of the silent troops.

These people who have shared their stories — and many whose stories are not recorded here — were all my tutors. I learned from the angry as often as the serene, from the passive as often as the aggressive, from the pessimist as well as the optimist, from the young as well as the old. I was as often a reluctant learner as I was a willing one, yet each person contributed in some way to my understanding that there are no recipes; there are no formulas; there are no pat answers. There is only hope.

The HOPE to Live Fully

The Patient's Story

"It is only to an individual that a soul is given."
A. Einstein

Each person has their own words for suffering and hope. Collectively they speak as if to say, "To understand that I am ill does not mean that you understand how I experience my illness. I am unique. I think and feel and behave in a combination that is unique to me. You do not understand me because you have a label for my disease or because some distant relative of yours died of it. It is not my disease or treatment that you need to understand. It is me. I am an individual. This could happen to you."

Illness is the great equalizer. There is no immunity by virtue of rank or privilege. Each of us is only a diagnosis away from being subject to the artificial separations between patients and the rest of the world. Each of us could be asked to wear the unbecoming hospital gown, to wear the wrist band for identification, to share a room with a stranger, to undergo invasion after invasion, to tolerate repeated, unintended indignities in the pursuit of recovery. Each of us could be the person who is left uninvited to the party, unnoticed in the flurry of "normal" activities. Each of us could be the person that someone else thinks is dying. Each of us is potentially "the Patient."

In reality each of us is vulnerable. To what specifically, we may not know as yet. Until then, our reactions are simply conjecture. Until then, we can live only vicariously the suffering and the resilience of the human spirit through those we call "patients." The patients in the next pages tell of their struggles, their triumphs, their fears, their humanness.

Each of these stories is a statement of the unique way in which people meet their illness. Their stories give us permission to approach our challenges in different ways, with individual strengths. They remind us that there is no "right" way. Their stories are as much a comment on our lives as theirs. Each story can be the gift of a mirror through which to view our own lives.

These people, and the many others whose experience I have come to respect so deeply, are feeling more, thinking more, fighting harder, caring more, expressing more than those of us who have the option of complacency in our lives. They are LIVING with disease. They know life can be threatened. They have ceased to live with the illusion that life is endless and that there will always be time to do what we fantasize we want and to be who we think we really are. They have conversed with despair and courted hope. They have come to understand what it means to be vulnerable and human.

"I can't often measure progress on a daily basis… I do it by the hour."
— Stan

STAN

Hope: The Courage to Go On

Scared. I am still scared. I still have the fear of death. I still have the fear of simply sitting in a wheelchair and having my whole body deteriorate. That could still happen to me.

I have lots of things going for me, though. I am back up on my feet now. I can think of how much I've been through, and how strong I am, and how able I am to survive. And that helps some.

There were ugly times, times when I couldn't do anything but lie flat in bed, when I hardly even knew what was going on. They were really terrible. In spite of those, the struggle is worth it.

It's a long ways back... the distance back is sometimes very hard to put in perspective. The only way I can do it is to look back where I have been. "I've come this far in the last two weeks. I've come this far in the last month. I've come this far in the last two months. I've got to get to the next step." That can be very hard to do. I can't often measure progress on a daily basis. Matter of fact, I seldom can. I do it by the hour.

I grasp for the physical things because they're more specific. It's easier to measure progress that way — easier to make comparisons and measurements. With the lethargy, the weakness, the radiation symptoms, the spinal damage, each day is a little bit of a struggle. If I can go to the kitchen, if I can reach something or take something out of the refrigerator or make something for myself or do something that I couldn't do a week ago, I feel I am progressing.

A few months ago, the wheelchair terrified me. I thought, "What a horrible thing to be in a wheelchair!" I found out that the wheelchair released me from the prison of being in bed all the time. Then I hated the walker because it was an appendage I had to take along with me all the time — but it got me free of the wheelchair. I looked at my two canes, and I thought, "I don't want to walk with two canes. I'll look like a goddamn freak." Now the two canes free me from the walker. Maybe the two canes will be a step to one cane in a while.

If I can accomplish something physical, like walking a distance and walking fairly normally, with a normal stride and gait, that seems to help quite a bit, even though some days I have so much lethargy and inertia that I don't even want to try. I don't like a whole day of feeling crummy and not being able to do anything, but I do have them. I'm impatient with them. I try to balance the amount of impatience against the necessity of having to rest.

It's important to have goals, but the upsetting part is to have the goals and not be able to meet them. It's a little demoralizing. I like the days when I can walk all the way down the street and back in the sunshine and come in and say, "Oh, I had a real good workout, and it'll be good for my balance and my muscles." I can go and lie down then and feel I haven't wasted the time. Those are the relatively easy days.

For the most part, I have a strong will that comes from inner depths. I don't really know where it comes from. I have fantastic family support from friends and acquaintances. That's the source of most of my strength. Of all the people I talk to and all the people I see, there isn't one of them who doesn't give me something. I think I take a little bit of strength from every one of them, and I don't think it diminishes them. It may even strengthen them.

It makes my day when someone comes because they want to see *me* … because I am Stan, not because I am sick. That's the most important thing. People at the hospital help a lot. I find that most of the staff there are just outstanding. After four years, dozens of them know my name, dozens of them stop me and say, "Gee, you're walking better," or "You're doing better," or "You're coming along," or "How are you?" They always seem cheerful, and that encourages me. It's very important.

It's important to recognize people's limits. Certain doctors can only think in terms of the disease as a malignancy. They can't see the patient as a person. They can't see any of the other things that interfere with a patient's struggle to recover and survive. Some of them don't understand that I am not the same. Everything is changed. It is not only a person's *body* that is affected. I'm not as cheerful as I used to be. I don't smile as easily. I'm a little more short-tempered. My role as a breadwinner, a husband, a dad — that's all different. That's hard. My perspective has changed. What I valued hasn't changed, but every little thing that's positive is important. Everything that is close personally is more important.

I want to give back to my family in particular. This whole thing is stressful on them. I don't know how to avoid it. I don't know how to relieve the pressure. One of the ways I can give back is to do my best to get better. That puts an extra burden on me, but it also helps me to remember that I've got to try physically, and I've got to try in every way to improve every day.

The only thing I know to do is to keep fighting and keep struggling. I've seen people who didn't. Maybe there was no struggle left for them. I'm not sure. I will never know. I just know that in the time I have, I want to be able to live something resembling a normal life. I want to spend time with my family without them feeling that I'm an invalid, that I'm a drag on the family. I want to see my boys grow up. I have a lot of things I want to do. I'm not ready to die, and I'm not ready to become a total invalid.

"I finally determined that, just because I was sick, I wasn't going to stop living."
— Murray

MURRAY

Hope: The Challenge to Begin Again

My whole life changed in twenty-four hours. I went in at four o'clock in the afternoon, and fifteen minutes later I was diagnosed. I was told to go home, pack my clothes, and be at the hospital in the morning for surgery. Nobody tells you anything! They say, "You've got cancer. Be in the hospital tomorrow." I was asking myself, "Why me? I'm only twenty years old. How can I have cancer? What did I do wrong?"

People didn't know what to say to me. Some people couldn't even look me in my face. My younger friends wouldn't talk to me. Young people are so scared of it. Only older people would talk to me. By the time I got out of the hospital, I didn't have any friends anymore. They were all gone, except for one real good friend. I finally bought a parrot. He was the best friend I had at that time.

It was hard not being able to talk. One day I thought I was going to have a nervous breakdown. The whole world started spinning around. I was so scared I didn't know what to do. I'd never felt like that in my whole life. I was just terrified. I didn't know where I was. I didn't know whether I was going to be doing this for a long time or short time. They kept talking about "odds": "You have such and such a chance for surgery." "You'll never have kids." The whole place was closing in. I locked myself in the bathroom and started crying. There was nowhere to go and no one to talk to. I was scared of the unknown. I just didn't know what was coming.

I got really lucky, though. I met this fourteen-year-old kid with leukemia. We started talking. He had a really positive attitude. He didn't feel sorry for himself. He'd been going through this for a long time. I was feeling sorry for myself. He sort of kicked my butt. I read in the paper about three months later that he had died. He was an inspiration to me. He shook me up. They were telling me I could be cured. He knew he was dying, but he had a good attitude. He always had hope that something would change. He never gave up. It was just fate meeting a special person like that.

One day I said to the only other bald guy in the waiting room, "Can I talk to you?" He said, "Sure." I said, "I'm scared, man." We became really good friends. I asked him if he would come for a walk with me. He wasn't feeling very good, but he knew I was scared to death. We walked around and around. Anyone who walked in the door to visit, I took them for a walk. I could not calm down. I was too hyped up. The thing that bothered me the most was that nobody was telling me anything except the people I was meeting myself. People don't know what it's like to sit there with those bottles dangling. You're on chemo treatments twenty-one out of twenty-four hours a day. Your veins give out. They start talking about using the ones in your legs or cutting a hole in your chest. Your hair starts falling out. There is just too much happening to you. People don't understand what it feels like to eat soup and watch your hair fall in your bowl. That's really scary. You're sick and you're puking. You keep thinking, "God, what are you doing to me?" I lost my girlfriend, I lost my hair, I lost about forty pounds, I had ulcers in my throat, I had nothing. I was stripped of my dignity. I wanted to quit. They won't let you quit. I tried quitting. I said, "I don't care. I quit. This is it. I quit. I'm fed up with this. My whole life is falling apart." I had no rights, I had no emotions left. I just gave up. They could've killed me. I didn't care.

I finally determined that, just because I was sick, I wasn't going to stop living. I started to get back into shape. I was feeling good, I was putting on weight. Then they told me I had spots on my lungs. I just freaked out. I cried. The light at the end of the tunnel led to another tunnel. I was determined I was going to get out of there. That's when I started praying the most. The night before my biopsy, I prayed. I said, "Look I've been through enough. I don't want anymore, I can't take anymore." I went for x-rays in the morning. I asked to see my x-rays. The technician and I were looking at them. I said, "I don't see any spots." He said, "I don't see any either." They canceled my tests and told me I could go home. They said, "You're cured." Just out of the blue, I was cured. I could go home. I was done.

It was like having a celebration with no one at the party. I'd always envisioned it different. I thought I would walk out of there and think, "Yeah, I'm done, I'm out," and people would say, "Right On." But there was nobody there. There was no celebration.

My one friend took me to a bar. I was totally bald and skinny. I said, "You know, people are going to bug us." My friend's bald too! He's six feet, 220 pounds. He said, "If anybody bugs you, I'll just take off my hat." I felt really safe. Like I had a big brother.

I feel I went through it for a reason. After it was over, I thought it was the best thing that could've happened to me. It straightened out my thinking. I'm a stronger person. I have more motivation. I have more goals for myself now, and I have accomplished some of them. I have more drive. Nothing holds me back now. I have a real desire to make it. I want to enjoy life while I have the time. I was wasting time before. My whole life is starting fresh again.

I still hate insurance salesmen. Here's this obese guy, sitting in a chair who says, "You're a cancer patient. Your rates are going to go up."

My reaction is, "To hell with you, I'm healthier than you are any day." I don't care what they say, I get so mad. Who are they to tell me I'm not good enough? Why don't people treat me like a person? I'm done with cancer.

"It's all worthwhile when you have a family you're darn sure loves you."
— Myrtle

MYRTLE

Hope: The Blessing of Family

I was born in Saskatchewan on a farm. My mother and one brother died when I was fifteen. I helped my father and five of my brothers on the farm for several years. It was hard work. There were no conveniences. We had to carry water from wells and scrub the floors by brush. But we didn't feel it was too much of a hardship; we enjoyed our life.

I married when I was twenty-two. There was no big fancy wedding or anything. It was hard times. My husband had been married before. His wife had died and he had two sons. We had a little boy, and the older boys loved and pampered him and spoiled him rotten. He died of meningitis when he was thirteen months. Two years later we got Allen. They all grew up to be very special boys. There was no difference among them. That was the most wonderful thing about step-children, seeing them grow up as one family. The three boys have given me more pleasure than anything else I can think of.

Later my husband bought grain for a period of time, and we had a restaurant in High Prairie. It was a big job, but I kind of enjoyed it. I guess it was the way I was raised, always feeding people. I loved to cook. My husband died there.

Life changed quite a bit after that. For a couple of years I was out in the bush cooking for the oilmen. There would be anywhere from ten to fifty men, and I had one helper. After that I lived with my boy Norman and helped him with his children until he remarried. They thought it would be nice if I stayed for a while, but I felt it was time to go to the senior citizens' home.

I have seen a lot of sickness in my time. I think of a sick body like a machine with a part that's not working just right. That doesn't mean the machine is no good. You just take out the broken part and the machine is repaired. Once when a doctor asked me about surgeries, I said, "Do you want to hear about all of them?" When I finished he said, "They didn't leave a darn thing for me to remove."

It was hard to take when I lost my sight because I love reading more than any other entertainment. Reading was my greatest pleasure, and I lost it overnight. Blindness is hard to take, but I believe you can get used to that, too. In a way it was harder though than the cancer. I am thankful I am not totally blind. I can manage a few things.

The last thing that happened to me was I found a lump in my breast. I would have been much more worried if it hadn't been for my very precious daughter-in-law. I think she was the one who helped me through it more than anything else. I wasn't such a bad patient, but it would have been terrible without her.

It was scary. I thought back on how many in my family had had cancer. My mother had cancer and she died. My grandmother had cancer and she died. My daughter-in-law had cancer and she died. My brother had cancer and he died. It made me kind of scared. I didn't really panic, though. I didn't dwell on it because I didn't have time. It helped a lot that I didn't have to spend a lot of time waiting.

They sent me home three days after the surgery. I don't think that was right. It was too fast. I had an infection, and I was pretty sick there for a while. I think that's the only time I ever felt I was sick. They didn't really seem to help me too much. Then I got a blood clot in the lung. I think that scared me more than the mastectomy.

I had such an awful time persuading them that I was in pain. Then they found this blood clot and they got busy! It took months to recover.

I still wonder if the surgery was the right decision. I can't really know. It's hard to know when you are over eighty. I just had to go ahead and pick.

I never really gained my strength back. But there is no point in moping and crying. It just makes a person unhappy, and it makes everyone else unhappy. It's not easy getting old, but I haven't really minded. I think my eightieth birthday was as nice a birthday as I've ever had. It was just about as good as when I turned twenty-one. All my children came to see me. It's all worthwhile when you have a family you're darn sure loves you.

"There was supposedly no hope for me."

— Russel

RUSSEL

Hope: The Lived Legacy

I had been a workaholic. I stayed in the oilfield for thirty years because I loved it. It was just my thing. I started at the bottom and worked my way up. I worked seven days a week, all kinds of hours. But when they diagnosed pancreatic cancer, it all came to an end. The doctors recommended I quit work, and I haven't worked since. They figured I would last about six months. That was over six years ago.

We were told there was a good chance I might never survive the surgery. I knew the whole thing was dangerous when my family came to see me. I have three sons. The oldest two are out on their own, and the youngest, who is mentally handicapped, lives with his mother. My sons were calm on the outside, but I knew they were upset. They love me a lot, but they are not the kind to say, "I love you," or to put their arms around me.

In surgery it was decided taking out the tumor was too risky. They never did touch it. They did a couple of bypasses, hoping it would make things easier if the tumor blocked off the ducts from the pancreas to the jujeum. Then they closed me up. I got radiation therapy. That doctor gave me a better prognosis. I asked him how long people lived with this type of thing, and he said the longest they had was a guy who lived five years. Things seemed a little brighter.

The doctors don't know how long the tumor is going to lie dormant. It still shows up on the ultrasound. All I take is pancreatic enzymes. I worry off and on at times. It's harder when I'm waiting for the results of tests. What's it going to be this time?

As a person, I am kind of private. I realized I might not survive, but there was no use crying about it. It wasn't going to stop because I cried about it. I cried, but not for long. I was never one to lose control. I never went through that period of "why me?" that others seem to have. When

I got this, I guess I said, "That's life and I'll deal with it." That was what I was taught to do.

My father was a farmer and a horseman. He went blind later in life. One day when he was elderly he leaned over the fence to pet a favorite horse, and he fell backward onto his neck. He was seventy-five years old and paralyzed. I watched him take seven-and-a-half months to die. My mother sat beside him every day and never believed he was going to die until the day he did. I don't know if he ever believed it. He was told he would never handle the pain and that he would lose his mind before he died. He never gave in. He was proud of that.

My mother is phenomenal, too. She loves life. She is ninety-five and gets disgusted and angry with people who don't live life to the fullest and who don't appreciate opportunities to do things and to keep going, no matter what's happening in their lives, no matter what the circumstances. Three years ago she broke both arms and fractured one side of her neck when she fell down a flight of stairs. Until the family got involved, the doctors weren't even going to set her arms. They did and she is totally well now. She crochets every day. She plays cards. She has a memory that is remarkable. She still to this day says, "Live life, don't whine and carry on." My brothers don't believe in whining either.

The worst part has been learning what to do with time without being at work. I was used to being with a lot of people. I had to develop other interests. It was much like a forced retirement. My wife wasn't used to having me around. Initially, it was okay because we wondered if I was going to survive, and we spent every minute as if it was precious. When things settled down, we had time to get on each other's nerves. It's not because we didn't love each other. It's because people still need time away from each other. It's impossible to be everything to another person. My wife acknowledged she was mad as hell that our lives had to change. She claims I have helped her through that just by being strong and by being patient, just by saying, "This is what we have to do, this is the way I want to live. I want to fight this disease, and we will do what we have to do."

CanSurmount* has helped. My wife went first. At that time I didn't feel I wanted or needed that kind of help. It was about two years later before I started to go to the group. It's good to talk to other people. When I see someone else I can help a little bit, it takes my mind off my own problems. I think I've got problems until I meet people who have more problems. Now I talk to other patients and tell them there was supposedly no hope for me. Maybe that helps someone.

We both appreciate life a lot more now. Just being alive gives me joy. I don't really have a list of things I want for the rest of my life. Just to be with my family. In a way it's been a really good experience. But I wouldn't rush out and wish it on anyone.

---

*A self-help cancer support group.

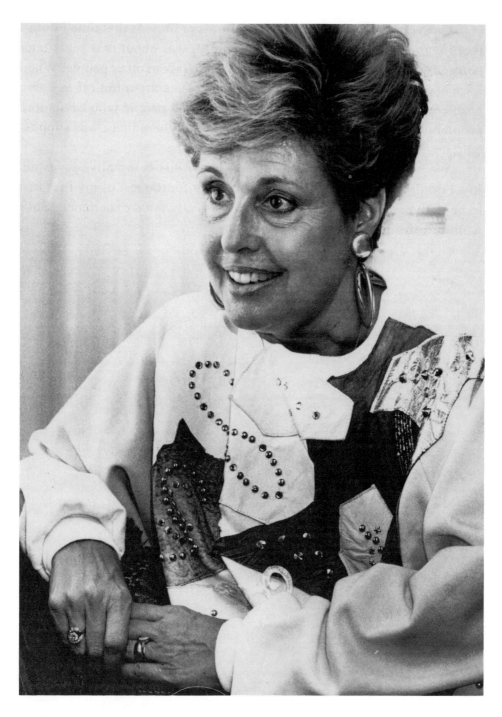

"Gradually I am becoming confident that I can face whatever the future holds."
—Joan

JOAN

Hope: The Challenge to Conquer the Fear

I was trying to be super everything. Supermom. Super volunteer. Running eight different directions at one time, trying to keep the house, make meals, drive the kids to lessons, and heaven knows what else! I was absolutely burning the candle at both ends. Probably one of my greatest challenges was converting to Judaism. I think once I converted, I set out to be a Super Jew.

I was like that as a kid. I hated to be left out if something was going on. I wanted to be there and be part of it. When I became involved, I felt less insecure. There is a basic insecurity that has been a big thing in my life. I was very sensitive and hurt easily. I never really talked to anybody about my real fears. If I kept myself busy enough, I could avoid having time to reflect on what I was doing.

I always seemed to be able to make things stressful, simply because of time management. I would end up without enough time to do all the things I had to do because I'd procrastinate. It worries me because I think there is a relationship between stress and cancer. Now every time I have a stress, I think, "Oh my God, there goes my immune system."

It's been seven years since my biopsy. My doctor told me right away that this lump he had been watching for three months was definitely malignant. The most difficult thing, which I am still not facing, is that it had spread to my lymph nodes while I was being watched. What sticks in my mind more than anything is the fact that I should have known better than to trust the mammogram and a fluid biopsy. I can come to grips with having breast cancer, but it is hard to come to grips with it having spread. That is still a hurdle for me. The fact that I cut my chances by so much in that three months! I can't say that I blame my physician. He did what was being done at the time.

Before cancer, I would say I led a superficial life. I don't regret the change. It's unfortunate that I had to have cancer to make the change. I still have a long way to go.

I think that my life is important enough to fight for. Somehow I have decided that maybe I am not so bad as I thought I was. I don't know how to put it. I have a lot more confidence in what I can do. If things bother me, I talk about them. I scream at hockey games. That part of me doesn't worry about what people think. That part of me wants to be free to be me, to do what is natural. I am a demonstrative person. I'm a hugger. I guess it is conduct unbecoming to my age, but I hate having this matronly age creeping up where it suddenly doesn't seem acceptable to do those things.

I have found myself becoming friendly with a whole different circle of people over the last six years. Before my surgery, I was always too busy to be bothered. Since surgery, I've taken time to meet people. It is important that I have a friend that I can talk to, like my friend Gracie in Hawaii.

I attended a cancer support group. There was a strength in the group that I couldn't put my finger on. We were all suffering. There was a common bond that we all shared that gave us strength to keep going, even for those who didn't make it. Before the group, I don't think I could have even faced talking to someone I knew was dying. All of a sudden I seemed to be able to do that. It's kind of like we're all dying in a way — the day we're born we start to die. The time is just different for each of us. I remember the group leader coming in with a message from Carol, who had just passed away: "Tell the group, 'It's okay.'" Carol hadn't been part of the group long, but the group must have given her something in the short time she was with us. This sort of fellowship was so strengthening. I am really "cheesed off" with government budget cuts because now there's no more support group. My social group just doesn't understand in the same way.

If people don't understand, they say the wrong thing. One of the wrong things to say is that you understand when you really don't. I was out for dinner, and I happened to meet a chap who had been a childhood friend with whom I had become reacquainted in the last few years. It was shortly after my surgery, when I was undergoing my chemotherapy. I was coming into a restaurant, and he called me over to his table. He asked, "How are you doing?" I said, "I'm doing just fine. I'm on chemotherapy right now and having no adverse effects." He turned to me and asked, "Would you mind not talking about that? I can't deal with that right now." I thought afterward, "Why ask?" It is like people are asking, but they don't really want to hear. That bothers me. It ends up being easier to say, "Oh, I'm fine," than to say, "I've had a bad day" or "I'm feeling a little tired from the chemotherapy today." They don't really understand. Some people say to me, "Ah, you're going to live longer than I am. You're going to outlive me." That's not what I need to hear. What I need to hear is, "Yes, I know you are scared and I am scared for you." The fact that I might outlive someone is irrelevant. It's the fact that I live with fear while they don't.

The fear is still there. And not only the fear, but the fear of how I'll react if the cancer does recur. What strength am I going to have if it does? How will I handle the sense of injustice if it does? It is something over which I have no control. The not knowing is hard.

No matter how you look at it, having cancer is an "alone" experience. No one else can deal with it for you. It's like an image I had in a relaxation class one day. I was in a boat by myself. (I am afraid of water!) I had a sense of wondering what I was doing alone in the middle of the water with no visible means of moving anywhere. I was not aware of oars or sails. Yet I had no fear. The image made me question if I had some fear that I would be abandoned. I think it's more likely that I am gradually conquering my own fear, gradually becoming confident I can face whatever the future holds.

"I can't imagine living without hope."

— Pat

PAT

Hope: The Awareness of Many Blessings

I wanted straight information. I said. "If you're not prepared to give straight talk, then you're wasting my time and I'm wasting yours and I'm leaving." And I would have, too. He looked quite sad and said, "Pat, I'm quite sure it's a malignancy." He added, "I'll leave the door open one percent."

I was quite calm. I couldn't believe how I felt. My main concern was my husband and my kids. And my friends. I knew they were going to be upset.

My husband, Norman, was very supportive in everything I wanted to do. When you have been married as long as we have, you know each other pretty well. I really didn't need the words. He was there. I knew he was absolutely there. That's what counted to me. He'd come by me and just put his arm around me and give me a hug. He said he was sorry. He wished it could be different.

We've been married forty years this summer. We have always been a couple that can look across the room and by moving an eyebrow, or a little grin or wrinkle of the nose, we know what the other person's thinking — in a crowded room. We've had a good marriage. Sure, we've had some ups and downs. There isn't a marriage that hasn't. (If there is one, it must be deadly dull.)

I didn't always have a sense of humor. Perhaps that's because I am the eldest. Norman has the most marvelous sense of humor. He's taught me the humorous side of things, whereas I tend to look on the downward side. It didn't take me all that long to catch on.

When I heard that I had spots on my skull, I asked the doctor, "Wait a minute, what's this about spots on my skull? Why was I never told about this?" He said, "I'm sure you were." And I said, "I'm just as sure that I wasn't. I've been told that I had holes in my head before, but now you've got proof I want to see!" And he showed me.

In less than a year it has become widespread. I don't dwell on it. I figure there is no point dwelling on these things, otherwise I think they could really weigh me down. I've had a fair amount of illness in my life, and I always feel that if they have done everything possible, then I have to go on with what I have.

I don't know how I will deal with it when it gets worse, which I'm sure it will. I am just being realistic. I know that I can deal with these things, and I can come out a better person if I work hard at it. Sometimes it's not very easy.

I count what blessings I have. I always have Norman. I always have his firm belief in me. Having faith and strong friendships are the other great pluses. Having a grandchild has given me an extra something to live for. I look forward to seeing her grow up. I don't know how long I'll be able to watch her grow. None of us do. I'm not saying that just because I have cancer. None of us knows from one day to the next.

I always have had my church. I've always felt that God is there. I find myself talking to God constantly. As far back as I can remember, I've been saying, "Now God, why this?" or "Well, you know, God, this is coming up and we need a little bit of help." I feel no need to go to church every Sunday. I think people are what they do with their daily lives. We are here to help one another. I firmly believe if we help but one person along the way, then we have done what we have been put on earth for. It doesn't have anything to do with denominations. I learned that volunteering in a cancer hospital.

Working there certainly helped me to be hopeful. It made me realize I grouched and complained unnecessarily sometimes. It made me look at life quite differently. I came to appreciate how fortunate I was to wake up each morning, relatively well and very loved.

It isn't easy to have cancer myself, but I don't believe that because you are told you have an illness that probably will be terminal, you should lose all hope. Why should you lose hope? If you lose hope, you might as well sit back in the rocking chair and say, "I'm gonna' die tomorrow." You have to have hope. I can't imagine living without hope.

"Music has a different place in my life now."

— Joan

JOAN

Hope: The Gift of Living in the Now

One thing that should be made clear is that endometrial cancer has a very good recovery history. I was never in any really life-threatening situation. That may have affected the way I reacted. On the other hand I think that, given the fact that no one really knows (at least at first), everyone must feel equally threatened when diagnosed, so my reactions may not be much different than they would have been if I had been diagnosed with lung cancer.

Cancer patients tend to talk about the importance of having a will to live. I don't have any great determination to survive. I am relatively happy, I have no unfinished business, like young children who need me, but the future isn't necessarily something I look forward to.

When the doctor said, "I have serious news for you," I laughed a lot. I thought, "This is the funniest thing I have ever heard." I tend to think of life as being a bizarre joke in many ways. It didn't occur to me to think, "Why me?" My relatives have all lived to be about a hundred, and the most depressing thought I had entertained up to that point was the thought of growing old and incapacitated.

My first urge was to tell everyone I saw. Then I wanted to know more. The doctor had said to call him if I had questions, but I had no idea what questions to ask. I imagined the cancer racing through my body, and I wanted to start treatment that day or sooner. I never did want to read books, though. When I did get a more detailed explanation from the oncologist, I was quite satisfied.

I tried to put my life in order: check my will, insurance policies, things like that. And I did feel the need to keep up a front. I think it's harder on others who are close to you, so I didn't want to be seen to be upset. Just once I felt really alone. I was waiting for my first implant. When my daughter left, all of a sudden I thought, "Poor me. I have no husband, no person to look after me or commiserate with me." I have no idea what I did to counteract that feeling. It didn't last.

I didn't like being in the hospital. There was a sense of being in a prison. I made escapes. I escaped over to the university. I went for a beer with my son. I didn't like people ordering me around. When I was quite weak and couldn't keep anything in my stomach, I was told, "You must walk." "All right," I said, "I'll run." I ran through the maternity ward and through the nursery. When my son came, the nurse explained I had taken off running down the hall. He said, "You don't understand my mother." At one point a nurse came in with an intravenous needle and said, "Well, here's your dinner." I asked, "Why? What's wrong? Who decided this? Why are you putting me on intravenous?" I wanted to talk to the doctor, whoever that was. "But," they said, "we can't get him, he's left on holidays." I replied, "If I don't hear from him by 4:30, I'm eating a huge meal." Eventually at 5:30 someone came. I told him, "I just had pork chops, gravy, mashed potatoes, corn, and a piece of pie. If I die, it's too bad."

When I was sick, I felt no sense of community with other patients. I was friendly, as I would be friendly with a well person, but I didn't feel in any position to reach out to them. I couldn't contend with their illnesses as well as mine. Even now it isn't easy. As long as I'm living in the real world, with real people who have all kinds of different problems, I would rather be part of that world than the world which has disease as its boundaries. I do some work for the Cancer Society now. If I can be helpful to people in bringing them back to the real world, as opposed to the world of cancer patients, then I am quite willing to enter the world of illness, but it is not my world. Some people, I feel, have made the world of illness their real world.

When you reach your forties, you tend to ask, "What have I done so far? What's to become of me?" A person who thinks, "I have chosen a career, and my career will continue to crescendo until I retire," is going to find out that that isn't really what happens. Even if you can't be drummed out, you can be cast back to the bottom of the heap. Your self-esteem can be shattered. The future, which seemed so obvious, is suddenly not what it seemed. As a professional musician, I was particularly caught in a bind. I realize one shouldn't go by what other people think, but in music that's what counts: You're measured by the opinion of others.

During treatment, it was nice not to think about things — just to live one day at a time. Recently, when I was waiting for the results of a biopsy, I realized I was back in a nice parameter of thinking about immediate things and not about the future. When I found out everything was all right, I felt a sense of relief, but in another sense, I didn't have that nice immediacy any more.

Music has a different place in my life now. I played in the Edmonton Symphony for twenty-three years. I still play professionally, but I enjoy it in a different way — it's hard to explain. I play at weddings and in a concert band that just made its second record, and I have a little jazz group. We play at wine and cheese parties.

Listening to music is important, I think. You can sort out things that you don't sort out when you're actually experiencing them. It focuses your feelings. Sometimes in my life I don't feel anything very strongly. At other times I feel things far too much. When I was in the hospital, I found Zamfir's record "The Lonely Shepherd" very tranquil and calming. Once a long time ago when I was really depressed, all I could listen to were those absolutely awful evangelical hymns, like "The Old Rugged Cross," with the simple I, IV, V, I harmonies. Anything else was too poignant. I can see why those hymns appeal. I remember that when my dad's sister died, he and I talked very matter-of-factly about her death. Then he said, "Why don't you put on Brahms' Alto Rhapsody?" It was only then that he became emotional. Music can do that.

"Just take it as it comes and don't sweat it if you can't know what's coming down a month from now."

— Dave

DAVE

Hope: The Challenge to Meet Everyday Losses

I had worked at clearing brush at the lake, and at the end of the day I couldn't lift anything else. The doctor looked me over and thought I was a little overweight and said, "Maybe you could cut out coffee, and here is a book with some back exercises that you can do to strengthen your lower back. If it doesn't clear up in a couple of weeks, come back and see me." A couple of weeks later I went back.

It really didn't sink in for a long time. No one actually said the word, "Cancer." My doctor always spoke in terms of "Multiple Myeloma." He said, "This might cut your life short a little bit, but you know you're good until fifty-five or so." I found that pretty encouraging.

The amazing thing is that I was diagnosed and undergoing treatment for about two years, and I had never been in the hospital overnight. There were some tense times, though. All the tests seemed to be on Thursday or Friday, and the results would never be in until Monday or Tuesday, so there seemed to be a lot of weekends that were full of anguish.

Hospitals are strange places. When I get out of one, I feel better just having freedom. If I feel like lying down, I can lie down. If I feel like having a snack, I can go and do something about it. In the hospital, you follow their regime. "It's ten o'clock, it's time to take pills. Are you sleeping at ten o'clock? Well, wake up and take the pills!"

They'd always draw blood between 7:30 and 8:00 a.m. With my blood I'd end up holding my arm for a half hour. Meanwhile, my tray'd be there for breakfast, and I'd be feeling sick to my stomach. I needed to get something into it, but I'd have only one hand to work with.

None of this was on purpose. The nursing staff was very encouraging. They always seemed to have a decent frame of mind. Even the caretaking staff was friendly, and you normally don't see that. Somehow I'd often get the same people cleaning my room every day.

I was in a room by myself a lot because of my blood count. In a way I liked it. I liked the quietness. A lot of the times I just didn't want to be bothered by other people. Part of it was not having a clear idea of my responsibilities. If the guy that's next to me was moaning and groaning, I'd wonder if it was normal for him. Should I call a nurse?

What gets to me is my inability to do stuff, my hesitancy to do stuff …like rake the lawn or shovel snow. I guess one of the frustrations is that other people don't place the same degree of importance on those tasks. It's very frustrating when I see a task and I can't do it. I don't stop wanting things done just because I'm not well enough to do them.

There are other things that are hard on my ego. I always cry the blues to people about having to look up to my wife, Arlene, now. She used to have to raise her head when we embraced. Now she doesn't. I started out 5' 9½", and now I'm pretty sure I'm less than 5' 4". It doesn't feel good when I see people I haven't seen for a long time, and I find myself looking at their navel. I drive a little Toyota truck, so I had to get a little cushion so I could see over the steering wheel. It's not good for the morale when you get to that point. I feel like I'm twelve years old, learning to drive. It's not a big deal when you get down to it, but I get a little depressed sometimes. There's always the lingering thought, "When is it going to run out?"

I don't know if I can describe explicitly the process that goes on in my head, other than to say I just take it as it comes. One fellow who had exactly the same thing as I did, even the same chemo, was dead in three months. For me, it's been five-and-a-half years.

I am kind of a private guy. It's always been a trait, and the onset of cancer hasn't really changed that substantially. Arlene and I don't talk feelings a lot. When you know each other, there can be support without talking about it. Caregiving and rescuing are a lot different. Rescuing can make the rescuer feel good, but it might not make the patient feel good. Arlene knows the difference. When times were tough for a while,

I'd want a pain killer before I'd even try to get out of bed. So she was there to get that. That's caregiving.

My sister has been my other main support. She tends to be nonjudgmental. If you ask her for advice, she can lay it on to you straight. During the diagnosis phase she was especially great. I could ask, "What are all the implications of this? This is what they are telling me. What might they not be telling me?" She has been our source of technical information.

I find that I have difficulty sometimes knowing how to respond to certain people. Somebody might say, "Well, how are you today?" They don't give a damn how I am. All they want to hear is that I'm fine, I'm okay, I'm reasonable. They don't want to sit down, and they don't want me to put my arm on their shoulder and say, "Listen, I've got all these damn problems. This is where I'm at with this, this, this, this, this. You know I've got rib pains, I've got back pains, I'm taking pain killers every once in a while. And I am plagued with leg cramps at night." They don't want to hear that. It's just a question of who is doing the asking and being able to interpret whether they really want to know or not. I found that it took me a long time to catch on.

In lots of ways I am really helpless, but there are things that I can do. I use positive affirmations. I believe in God and in Heaven. The affirmations, or you could call it prayer, help me at least to feel like I'm helping myself.

I don't think of myself as a survivor. Life has a kind of constant unknown factor. My motto is, "Just take it as it comes and don't sweat it if you can't know what's coming down a month from now." I don't think much about the future except when it comes to some financial things. I don't have a sense of being well again. I've kind of resigned myself to the fact that I won't be going back to work. In some ways I've been kind of a fatalistic person. When your number is up, it is up.

"I found out I can make an incredible difference in almost every aspect of my life."

— Del

DEL

Hope: The Need to Take Charge

I didn't have a lot of confidence as a kid. Being raised in a rural area, I wasn't very sophisticated. When I got out on my own, I started testing myself. First it was skiing, then karate, then body building. But there has been no test as tough as beating cancer.

I was diagnosed only six months after I had married Lynn. When I met her I went into overdrive! I suppose I have been supercharged about most things in life. Because I had been working so hard and had so many things going on, I had an explanation for each of the symptoms. The weight loss was from the exercising, the night sweats from drinking a protein drink at bedtime, the fatigue from my sixty-hour work weeks. When Lynn spotted the lump on my neck, there was no question something was wrong. I could tell that in the eyes of my doctor. In less than twenty-four hours, she had to tell me, "Del, we have bad news. You have two massive tumors in your chest." She said "tumors" and she said "malignant." I knew what that meant.

Our lives have never been the same since. In a lot of ways life is much better now, but getting this far has been an unbelievable challenge. Chemotherapy was the toughest part. I can remember sitting there on the first day. It seemed to take forever. I was nervous and anxious. A guy came into the room, grabbed a little pail, and started throwing up. I thought, "This is bizarre." I knew right then that attitude was going to be important.

I had lots of support. Lynn was right in there with me the whole way. My family was pulling for me. The guys at the office didn't say much, but I could tell they were feeling for me. My job was never in question, and I knew they really cared. I also knew that wouldn't be enough. I was convinced I would have to help myself, too. With the first treatment I only threw up once. Strange, as a little kid if I threw up, I got special care. But I knew I had to get out of the trap of feeling like I should be special if I was sick. I didn't want anything that might entice illness to stay. Instead, we rewarded me with a trip to the Dairy Queen for being such a good boy.

I did some reading on the importance of attitude, and with the second treatment I didn't throw up. I wanted to overcome the psychological side of things. I did more reading. I started listening to tapes. The itching was subsiding, my weight was stabilizing, the night sweats were nearly gone, work was good, chemo was okay.

Lynn practically dragged me to a support group. I felt I didn't have much in common with these people. I didn't want to accept how sick I was. We sat in the very last row, and I made jokes to Lynn throughout the presentation. I ended up getting superinvolved. I took the training sessions, talked to other patients, even ended up doing the coordination. So much for my initial reluctance. The group has really helped. Being involved gave me extra purpose.

Chemo was getting tougher, though. I was developing all kinds of psychological problems. I hit the library again. I felt I just had to counteract this or I would never be able to finish. I read a lot about the importance of a person's senses. I decided to go with the sense of smell from my childhood because of all the good memories of smells associated with my grandfather. I had always admired him. He was national rodeo champion in the twenties. In my eyes he was a real cowboy. He even chewed snuff. Every year we would spend a couple of weeks with my grandparents. One of the things that my grandfather did was to tan hides. I used to love the smell. So Lynn bought me a good pair of leather gloves. Whenever you rub oil on leather, the scent comes out. I dug out the suntan oil. It was a smell I associated with meeting my wife in Hawaii. Off I would go to the clinic with my little psychological bag: gloves, oil, Walkman, music. It helped, but I was always looking for more help.

I had heard marijuana would help. I knew that you had to build up a tolerance for it. The first time I got sick. I smoked for a week. The morning of the treatment I smoked it. Gee, I felt okay! If one makes me feel good, maybe I better have another one, just to make sure. That was icing on the cake, so I had another. I was so stoned, I was shaking. I threw up in the kitchen sink. Lynn scolded me, to say the least. She said, "Don't you ever use that again..." I was thinking, "Oh, thank God, I don't ever want to touch that stuff again." And I never did.

I tried all kinds of drugs, anti-nausea, anti-this, anti-that. They didn't do anything for me. The psychological stuff seemed to work best. I kept reading, kept listening, learned to meditate.

The whole deal was not as easy as I thought it was going to be. There was a point in the treatment where I thought, "I can't hack it." I actually went home and missed a treatment. Deep down I wanted to finish. I got some professional psychological help. I still had some anxiety in the next treatment, but the physical side effects were eighty-five percent better. I decided to get serious about this stuff. I got into a regime, learned to make my own tapes, made myself a positive charter that I read out loud every morning, even put it on video tape. I started to put weight back on. My hair started to grow back. I was back working. I was feeling good.

Then the itching was back. The tiredness. I was pretty scared. The tumors were back the size of oranges. Other guys were finishing chemo, and I was looking at starting again. I knew the numbers weren't in my favor this time. I stepped up my program. I read sixty minutes every morning. Mediated more. Put up a survivor poster. Told the physician I wanted active, not passive, treatment.

But, physically, I got worse and worse. I had deteriorated to the point where I was garbage. Mentally, I was getting stronger. I knew the fight was there. On the way to work in the morning, I would put on my headphones and listen to the greatest minds on the planet. When I got a lung condition, the radiotherapists were reluctant to treat me. One finally agreed. My blood counts were expected to interfere, but I worked on them with visualization. Much to everyone's surprise, I only had to postpone one treatment. There was still more chemo. I was getting pretty weak. We used to call how I walked the "chemo shuffle."

Things turned ugly at one point. My lungs got worse. I ended up on oxygen. I had to do some soul searching. "Am I going to get better or am I just going to die here?" That night I seemed to go downhill. The medical situation worsened. My veins were nonexistent. My blood was dropping off. I was having trouble staying oriented. They had to put in a catheter. I couldn't even reach my cassette player. The next morning something was right. The head of the clinic came in and said, "I think you have turned a corner." Ten days later I was out of hospital.

That was two years ago. I think we've made it.

Lynn and I were a team right from the beginning. It's great when you have a best friend, but it's even better when your best friend and your wife are the same person. She encouraged me. Right from the start she said, "You're a fighter." It was tough on our relationship. Our friends were all working on their careers, getting their education; they could party. Lynn was watching me physically slip away right in front of her eyes. She didn't know if she was going to be married or if she was going to be a widow. It must have been incredibly difficult for her.

She had to find that balance between caring for me and babying me. She recognized that I needed to stay in charge of my own life, that the responsibility for my life was ultimately my own. I think accepting responsibility is the key. No one can control everything, but I found out I can make an incredible difference in almost every aspect of my life.

The HOPE to Care

The Caregiver's Story

"You have touched me; I have grown."

I began my work at the Cross Cancer Institute assuming I, like the many dedicated people I joined, would make a difference in the lives of patients and families. I did not understand the difference they were to make in mine. The day came, as I imagine it has for many, when I was faced with the awareness that staying later, working harder, running faster was not enough. I had to deal with the unwelcome awareness that the task is endless, the challenges relentless. I stood at the crossroads of how to deal with powerlessness: resign or reconcile. Compromise was unappealing. It would mean that in distancing the sense of powerlessness, I would have to distance the patient. The signs are easy to spot. There is a movement toward those things over which one can exercise control: paper, schedules, treatment plans, research protocols; away from difficult questions, ambiguous answers, existential confusions. I knew for me distance was not the answer. It was on that day that I began to envision how caring *could* be.

I came to understand the first difference must be in my "Self." Each time I am insensitive, each time I fail to see a patient or a colleague as a unique person with their own thoughts and feelings, each time I am negative, the disease wins a little. Each time I convey respect, engender trust, encourage authenticity, or share laughter, my life and those lives it touches are a little richer. I never again had a discouraging day at the clinic. I never again measured success on the basis of a day, or even a month.

In preparing this section of the book on "caregivers," I chose not to interview the uninspired, few though they be. I chose people who demonstrate and share a vision of how caring could be. Each perhaps has their own version, but the difference lies in the means, not in the goals. Collectively they are a tireless movement directed to excellence in human caring.

"A real connection happens almost without words…at the heart level."
— Alice, nurse and clinical coordinator of support services

ALICE

The Hope to Make "Real" Connections

I can remember the first patient who said, "I'm going to kick the bucket, aren't I?" I just stood there. What do I say to this man? He's right. I didn't know what to say, so I just played deaf. I am a much better nurse now.

It never seriously occurred to me to be anything other than a nurse. How else would I be like Grandma? Every night she rode her bicycle to work at the nursing home where she looked after the elderly and dying people. She didn't tell me much. But I had this feeling that what she did was wonderful.

Losing her was very painful, even though I was an adult. As she was dying, I loved her so much. I loved every wrinkle on her face. I loved the gold in her teeth. Her smile. Her sparse hair. I wanted to be there for her. It was a beautiful experience. She had had fifteen operations in seven years. I remember crying and saying, "I don't want you to leave, Grandma. I know you're going to die, and I don't want you to. I'm not ready to let you go." She said, "I can tell that you don't want that." She'd say, "Sing some hymns for me." Wow. So I'd sit there and sing. "In the Garden" was her favorite. I often think about Grandma "walking with me"... how she'd feed the ducks. She was so special, it was painful to let go. She was probably the most important *real* connection I ever had.

A real connection happens almost without words. There *are* words, but the real connection happens at the heart level. When I have a real connection, I feel satisfied. I feel nurtured. I feel enriched. I have to be open for it without grabbing for it. I can't make it happen, because it takes two people. It becomes real when I don't have any expectations. I'm just open. It's a lot like I felt when I volunteered in Nicaragua. No meetings. No bureaucracy. No obligations. It was a matter of *being* together. That's how I handle dying patients. There is nothing more to do but *be* together.

I do what I can and what my patients will allow. Sometimes they have unresolved, unfinished business. It's not for me to decide our agenda, though. Something is important only if it is important to them.

As a nurse, my challenge is to find some common ground to share with a patient. Whether we're both Danish, have children, share a similar faith, enjoy crocheting, or love chocolate. That's not in the textbooks. You cannot have a deep connection with a patient without sharing. It's not a one-way communication. The *real* connections happen at the level of meaning. At that level, there is a sense that our connections have purpose — whether it's a time for reaching out or reaching in, a time for laughter or a time for tears.

The intensity is not always comfortable, but I find strength in an awareness that when I'm with a patient, I can call on something greater than myself. You can call it God, Spirit, Energy, Consciousness, Love. I call it God. When I have that awareness, I am able to do the simple things that matter.

If appropriate, I touch my patients. It might be only a quiet hand on the shoulder or forearm. Many of them will tell me they really miss being touched and the lack of touch increases their loneliness. I remember one man, a very educated man, I was looking after. He would sit in the chair and he'd lean forward, and I'd sit on the arm of the chair and just rub his back. That's how we'd talk.

A patient becomes my favorite as soon as our relationship allows them to become authentic. They're authentic when they are themselves — be that eccentric or angry, curious or depressed, sad or joyful. They are my favorite as soon as I get a sense they are congruent with the way they have lived. I know then that we trust each other. They just about all become my favorite.

One of my favorites was a marvelous fifty-seven-year-old Hungarian woman with a great zest for life who was angry as hell that she was dying. She didn't want to die and didn't want to talk about it. She was mad at God and was mad at everyone. I could hear her anger. I could feel her anger. I loved her more for being authentic. For being who she was. I could share her anger and distraughtness. I felt her struggling and fighting and wanting. We spent lots of times when I would just come and sit. We might talk or we might not. We might talk about kids. We might talk about husbands. We might talk about the leaves coming out, the rain, the weather. She'd look at me and she'd say, "Alice, I always feel better after you've been here. I feel like you are my sister."

I think of my task as that of facilitator. That is what we can do for each other. All of us. Whether it's patients or friends or family, we can just be together with each other in a facilitating way, with an open heart — open and accepting, without judging whatever the other person needs to share of themselves or is going through. I see this as the greatest gift we can give each other. Individuals within the medical system do it well, but the system itself doesn't. It can't, as long as it is controlling and patriarchal. How many people sit down and ask the patient, "What has all this done to you? What does this diagnosis mean to you? What has it done to your life? How does it affect your family? How is it affecting your sexuality? How is your spiritual life?" That's not happening.

If it happens at all, I think it will happen individually. I think it will come from you and me sharing with our colleagues, as we grow and learn, that we're able to be with patients and be that facilitator. And *really* hear them, cheer for them, give them information, share with them, help them see their options, their choices. I'm the hostess here, and the patients come for a visit. If we don't have that attitude, the patient is really in a prison.

"When the options have shifted, there's lots I can do to ease suffering."
— Neil, physician

NEIL

The Hope to Ease Suffering

I never regret for a moment my choice of career. I committed myself to medicine at twelve years of age. My older brother was already in medical school. My first job was delivering drugs on the back of my bicycle. It was the hardest work I've ever done in my life. I decided writing the prescriptions would be easier than delivering them!

Over the years I've seen a lot of people die. As a young physician with patients with acute cancer, I worked extraordinarily hard, putting in long, long hours, knowing my efforts were not going to be successful. I used to die a little with each patient. People who make an early choice for medicine tend to romanticize being able to heal all ills. I have a more mature and global sense of suffering now. I have a more philosophical recognition that I try my best.

Until relatively recently, physicians have rarely interrupted the trajectory of illness. Their role has been to assist with the alleviation of suffering. It's been for only a fairly narrow window in the twentieth century that we can, in fact, make a difference in the actual disease. Medicine still has its limits. In palliative care the goal is not cure. The challenge is to address the symptoms that cause the suffering. When I have to tell someone there aren't any more options, it's important that I do it from the point of view that the options have shifted. It's critically important never to close the door. There's lots I can do to ease suffering, even if it is extending a person's life for only a short period of time.

From my perspective the biggest difference in the last ten years in palliative care is the improvement in the management of pain. At the mechanistic level I have a far better appreciation of the drugs that can be used to help and what impact they will have on the patient. Part of the improvement still needed is to understand how to help with suffering.

Another extraordinary step is the recognition that a healthcare team has more to offer than one individual practitioner. Traditionally, there's a feeling of parentalism in medicine, which is good. In its most positive form, parentalism involves taking care of people and ensuring that their needs are looked after, but it has negative connotations because it tends almost to enroll patients as indentured servants. I think medicine tends to attract, by and large, "take-charge people" who have run into some extraordinary human problems at an early age. Part of their protective mechanism is to develop a take-charge personality. They do take charge, and they do become protective of their own turf. I don't know how that is taught in medical school, maybe to a willing personality type, but the message comes across fairly clearly.

The down side of my work is probably the family side. You can see the best and the worst of the family as a person approaches death. The worst thing I see is a family fighting with each other, failing to take responsibility for mutual support.

The up side, which far exceeds the down side, is the opportunity to work with remarkable families and patients. The ones I recall most vividly are the "redemption-in-the-face-of-anguish" type — those patients who, by background, appear to have been individuals of "little societal worth." They have lived their lives causing trouble for others and seem to have made little contribution to their community. Then they literally become saints in the course of their final illness.

I remember well a patient who died of acute leukemia. At the age of twenty-four, he had already been in jail for armed robbery and attempted rape. We plucked him out of a jail detention cell when he was diagnosed. There was nothing in his background that would suggest that he had a redeeming factor, but he became a source of extraordinary inspiration. We never got him into full remission during the three months he occupied a hospital bed. He had a very sparkling personality but was a very "tough guy." That combination endeared him greatly to the staff and was very helpful to other patients. He would go to their rooms and cheer them up. It was like having a permanent volunteer on the ward. I remember very well when we had run out of ideas. I had to convey very bad news to him. I was stumbling along, and he put his hand on mine and said, "Doc, look, I know what you're trying to tell me but relax, okay? I'm all right." He eased my suffering. When he died, there wasn't a dry eye in this hospital.

Our work is to serve the patient. I have been an administrator. In my view the administrator's role is to assist people in the trenches, who are actually working with the patients, to get their job done, and to make it easy for patients and their families to access the system. I am concerned about the increasing bureaucratization of medicine. I am concerned that we are establishing administration for its own sake. I think that has happened in hospitals to some extent. I suspect in some places that if all the patients were cured and left the hospital, it might be three years before the staff would realize, "Hey, there's no one here anymore."

As a dear friend in palliative care says, "Life is tragic, but not necessarily serious." We are small people, here for a while. The sands will soon cover over our seemingly important enterprises. Let's do our best, respect each other, and hope that someone's passage is the better for our existence.

"No matter how ill people are, I still need to give them the right to decide."
— Diane, palliative home care nurse

DIANE

The Hope to Be "Always a Guest"

I never planned on being a nurse. I had worked in a fabric shop, in a bridal shop, and in a school as a secretary. I was thirty-seven when I started training. When I applied, I was considered a risky candidate. It is something to go back to school after seventeen years. I paid my school parking fee for only one month at a time because I never knew whether I would hang in for the next month. My young classmates were super. The traumatic part was I had no peer. For my classmates the "people part" was most difficult. For me, it was the damn exams. Now, because I love it, I wish I had done it earlier.

When I started, team nursing was popular. The peer support was superb at that time. It was sink or swim. We had to work together. I remember coming home from a shift never even having looked out the window. We were often so busy with the "technical." It's frightening to realize how very easy it is to miss the "person."

I signed on with a homecare pilot project for a three-month session, and I loved it. You're no longer using a finely developed technical skill, and you are on the patients' turf. In a person's home you are allowed to do exactly and only what they want you to do. They'll often tell you just what they want you to know. You are a stranger coming in because they have lost their independence. It is difficult for them to accept that they can no longer get in and out of the tub themselves when not long ago they have been out mowing fields or raising kids. Sometimes people come across a little stronger because they've lost so much. They can be a bit difficult to approach.

I remember the first gentleman I went out to see. This man said to me, "Please sit down." He had the fattest, grossest dog sitting on his belly. I would have sworn the rug was a shag, but it wasn't. It was just dog hair. He was a chain smoker. He had cancer of the lung. He had coffee beside him and was on massive doses of analgesia. Right from the very first, it was established that I could only do what he would let me do, including "sit down." He would let me do a lot if I was gentle.

My standard of what I perceived as not sanitary had to do a swing around. My standard of what I thought was supportive had to be suspended. It wasn't appropriate for me to change a life style of habit. I couldn't make everyone the model family. It's impossible to be all things to all people. I was not there for that purpose. When patients are staying in an institution, the caregivers set the standards. But in the home, the patient sets the standards. I always ask, "Would it be all right if I come at such and such a time?" I am asking permission to go into that home.

One patient imprinted this lesson on me forever. She was in her forties, both her children were in elementary school, and the family was very supportive. Her tumor was wasting her from the inside out, so she still looked strong. I cared for her for nine or ten months.

She always had at least one extended family member with her. The community got together, and they set up a roster so that different ones came at different times. But even if someone stayed only ten minutes, if seven of them came, she would get exhausted. I saw such a lot of well-meaning love, but I learned that sometimes love needs to be directed. Everybody needs to do something, every family member needs a role.

The children helped. The little girls rubbed mom's elbows and hands several times a day with lotion. The little boy was asthmatic, so when I was in doing chest physio with his mother, we'd check his chest out at the same time. She also had a dog. He would sit right up beside her on the sofa and check out anything that was going on. The whole time she was saying she was going to "lick it." In her heart of hearts she knew she wasn't going to.

One time she hadn't voided for twenty-six hours, and her bladder was distended. She was very weak and very heavy to lift. I made some assumptions without asking her what she preferred. I thought it would be too exhausting to get her up, so I went ahead and catheterized her. Was she cross with me! I had just gone ahead without asking her permission. That was the nurse in me. I was simply doing a technical thing that I perceived had to be done. I learned from that experience: No matter how ill people are, I still need to give them the right to decide. It took a long time to repair the damage to our relationship. We had a lot of talks. I was even scared to go back because I knew I had been wrong. I was wrong for the right reasons, but I was wrong. I cried a lot when she died.

The deaths get to me at times. I remember my dad telling me, over a breakfast of greasy fried eggs and lots of butter on the toast, "Everybody is not dying, no matter what you think. Go and walk along the sidewalk, look at the buds on the trees, and try to keep things in proper perspective."

I hope I never forget, even for a moment, that the most important thing is that I see patients as people. First and foremost, I am working with a *person.*

"As I live more where the mysteries are, I still have my share of fear, but I am freer. My spirit can dance more easily."

— Graeme, counseling psychologist

GRAEME

The Hope to Dance More Freely

It is a given. We are going to die. We come to understand there is no choice. That is one freedom we do not have as humans. Where we *do* have a choice is in how we face death. In working at the Institute one comes to understand no matter how decayed the flesh, the spirit is present. No matter how horrifying someone may appear, we must honor them and their family. At some deep level we are committed to that.

People say, "It must be depressing working there." I don't find it as depressing or as discouraging as working with a healthy person. It's very inspiring. We see courage every day.

Each person faces a time of danger and a time of potential transformation. It's not for any of us to judge their response. It is for us to "be there" for them, not necessarily to "do" for them. The most stressful component is coming to terms with our own helplessness in dealing with very sick people whose hope is circumscribed and, who, it seems in the short term, are just losing on every score. In some cases just observing is a privilege.

I recall a Chinese gentleman who was very deeply philosophical and spiritual. He had arranged everything for his family. He was a city person, a businessman. He had done very well. He had done what he needed to do, and he had lived fully. Now he was going to die, and he died almost ceremonially and peacefully. He died very honorably and very cleanly somehow. He was one of the most peaceful men I have known. He calmed me down. I didn't help him.

I don't think it's possible to work with cancer patients and families without really questioning why you're alive, why you're living. It has changed my whole awareness of life. I used to think that a good life is a long life. If you can get your three score and ten, that's a privilege. I want that for myself, but I no longer see that as necessarily the ideal. The essential thing is the quality of time that I live. I don't know how that can be measured. I think it could possibly be measured in moments.

For me one of those moments was being at 13,000 feet behind Mt. Annapurna in Nepal, in a little temple that is both a Hindu and Buddhist pilgrimage point, listening to my Walkman play "Chariots of Fire" and just standing there watching the mountains. That was spectacular. That was one of those moments. I was almost overwhelmed with the beauty. Yet there was somehow also a sadness.

I don't think we can stand back and look at ourselves and our culture and the way we live in the world, raping the world, without feeling sad. I try to see life like a lake. The anger and the politics and the bitching and the back-biting and the stabbing and the conflict are all froth on the surface in a windy storm. The essence of humanizing comes from the deep, dark blue waters underneath. That's where the dolphins and the whales swim. That's where the mysteries are.

As I live more where the mysteries are, I sense a change in my spirit. I love more deeply. I appreciate more deeply. I bask in the sun more fully. I take time to smell the roses, to really see the sunsets. Likewise with my relationships. Looking from the top of Annapurna, the boundaries between me and everything else were a lot less clear. I felt connected with everything. I can't say I live from that spot very often, but I'm more aware of it. The biggest change in my spirit is that I am less afraid. I still have my share of fear, but I am freer. My spirit can dance more easily.

"If I am honest with myself, I probably get as much from the patients as they get from me."

— Paddy, physician

PADDY

The Hope to Live
What I Believe

From the age of twelve, I knew I wanted to be a doctor more than anything else. My middle brother and I were very close to each other, and he had just started in medicine. About the same time I read the book *The Story of San Michele* about a doctor who had his practice on an island in Italy. He describes his experiences during a cholera epidemic in Naples. I was very impressionable at the time. His story sounded marvelous. It appeared he had given his whole life to the sick and wasn't this wonderful!

I had an awful battle with my father about medicine. He just looked at the fees and said, "No way." In those days there were no student grants, but I eventually got a little scholarship. The way I got over my father's objection was to declare that my other ambition was to be a detective. I used to read all those Edgar Wallace novels, and I said, "If I don't do medicine, I'm going to become a detective." That swayed him.

I remember my first day in university. I just couldn't believe I was in the University of Edinburgh. The place was nearly four hundred years old. I was actually there and I was a student. I had no clothes, no money, no nothing. I was still in my school uniform, tatters of clothes, and my sister's hand-me-downs. I couldn't have cared less. I'd gotten there and it was the most marvelous day.

After years of married life and medicine in India and extensive training in Britain as a radiation oncologist, I was invited to come to Canada. A specialty in breast cancer was really accidental. I did research with Robert McWhirter, one of the first to say you don't need all this mutilating surgery. He was an absolute wizard at examining breasts. He taught me how to examine breasts, and it was a revelation. I ended up doing nothing but breast,

breast, breast, and I was becoming super-specialized.

When women initially come in for screening, they are anxious. When they come back for the first one-year recheck, I can hear them talking to the person sitting next to them, "Oh, I've been here before, you know." The best of the lot are the cancer patients who say, "What are you looking so worried about? I had the disease ten years ago." "You what?" They're marvelous for the waiting room.

I suppose it is easy for the ones who have accepted their predicament to become my favorite patients — the ones who realize I'm trying to help them, who understand that I have bad days, too.

I think I care more than I did in the earlier days. I'm told I have an honest face. It's an awful responsibility. If I wanted to, I could sell old rope as gold twine. But I think I can sell only what I really believe in, and I really believe in what I'm trying to do. I think that gets over to other people. I really do care.

I think I listen to people. I want to be sensitive to how they're reacting. Rather than getting aggressive back with the ones who are rude and aggressive — which is so easy to do — I appreciate that they are worried. In fact, if ever the receptionist is having a problem out front, I know it's somebody who is frightened. I am not unique. Basically, people who go into medicine are caring people, but they lose a lot of that with the pressure.

It is so difficult to decide who is denying successfully and who is really coping. There are people who will tell you they're fine, and then they have a complete breakdown a few months later.

It seems to me the older people cope better. I think they were brought up with a better philosophy of life. I guess it's like the way people react to all life's problems. There are people who accept and those who don't. I firmly believe that the older generation accepts more easily. Maybe it's because they lived through the bad times of the thirties.

I also think education helps. Fear and dread of the word cancer is more prevalent among the less well-educated. Cancer was a dirty word that wasn't even mentioned for many years. If someone's mother died very quickly of breast cancer when they were in their teens, they remember that and have an absolute horror of getting it themselves.

When I think of retirement, I think I would be terribly bored doing what I wanted to do all day long. If I am honest with myself, I probably get as much from the patients as they get from me. I do enjoy the patients, and I come home feeling I've done something to help people, which to me is what living is all about.

I have no idea about retirement. Nobody can anticipate, particularly at my age, how long their health is going to last. As long as I'm well, I suppose I will work. Perhaps I'll do more fishing.

Fishing is my relaxation. For me it's very, very regenerative. I just love getting out in the mountains. I always feel I'm right out of civilization when I hear the sound of loons. I like fishing on my own. The guide gets awfully worried. He says, "One of these days you're going to fall and hit your head on a stone, and you'll be lying there." I think, "Oh, what a wonderful way to die."

"I would just like to continue to grow, to give more."
— Naomi, friend to numerous cancer patients

NAOMI

The Hope to Be a Friend

I had had ulcerative colitis for fifteen years when I started going to support group meetings. It was becoming a mental battle with me. I was so sick of being sick. I was making myself sicker. Miriam insisted I start coming with her to relaxation classes at the cancer clinic. I didn't really know any of the details. I didn't know if I was really welcome. I didn't know if I really belonged. I felt mildly legitimate because I had been warned that, with my condition, I was a very high risk for cancer. So everything they were saying was very meaningful. It was to be a turning point.

In the five years since I began, I've come to think more of others than strictly about myself. I had tended to use my situation as an excuse for opting out of life. I learned so much from the people in the group. I found myself becoming friends with them outside of our relaxation class.

It was my great fortune to meet Jean in this group. She had the most profound effect on my life. She had so many strengths and so much warmth and so much love to give, even though she had so many heartaches and problems. I thought to myself, "She is one in a million. I wish I could be like her." I loved being in her company. Jean didn't do anything Jean didn't want to do. Initially, she intimidated me. I just sat totally mesmerized when I listened to her and thought, "Oh wow, I could never converse with this lady. I don't know what I'd say to her." That was the farthest from the truth. She was the easiest, loveliest person. The memories that really stand out are her genuine love and warmth and caring for people, and her absolute honesty with everything from emotions to the price of her car. That was refreshing. Now I find that whenever I am dealing with people in a situation and I reach a bit of a rough spot, or when I am a bit unsure, I think of what Jean would have done.

When I talk to the women in this group, I don't think in terms of illness. I think in terms of friends and people I really like. They have an illness, but other than that, they are really interesting, ordinary people. And I guess they need me just a little. It's not a test of any sort for me to be with them or to keep in touch. At some level I know they won't live to be ninety. I have one friend now who is quite ill. She makes it so easy to be with her. Sometimes we just sit out on her sun deck and talk. She typifies the other women in the cancer group. Their courage is extraordinary. They really see themselves as having no other alternative. They could become depressed and lie down and just have "poor me" days constantly, but they don't. When I think of the future for her, in my heart of hearts I just feel it'll take care of itself when the time comes. I hope to see her right to the end, much like we did with Jean and much like we did with Bessey and Donna.

Sure, it's really hard. But I saw Jean reach a sense of peace. She saw her daughter married. She saw two sons well on their way. Even the little things got done, like getting some small athletic embroidered things finished for her sons. Somehow I was able to say good-bye and still keep very alive. It wasn't the end of a life. There's still a relationship. I hope it will be much the same with Audrey. I make time each week. It has become a commitment.

I would just like to continue to grow. To give more. There's nothing truer than, "The more you give the more you get." I feel a whole lot better about myself because I am giving a little. I am just letting things happen right now. Jean would have said, "I'm going with the flow." I am not structuring goals, and I really believe things are just going to develop and happen. I hope I am smart enough to take advantage of them as they come along.

It is a privilege to share a difficult part of these women's lives. People not involved think of cancer as a death sentence. Maybe it is human nature not to want to be around sickness if you can avoid it. The impression I get from some people is, "How can you even go into that hospital if you don't have to?" People really don't understand what I am getting out of coming to the hospital.

Nothing has been more helpful to me than this group and the people I have met. They're not my social group on the whole, but somehow there is a common denominator. There is a basic sharing. They give my life meaning. It doesn't matter if you've got a big diamond or if you have a '54 Volkswagen. That's all irrelevant.

I am probably even more caring with my own family than when I was so into myself. I can speak more freely about my feelings now. I didn't have that gift. That is what Jean had. I guess that is what I loved about her so much. When she would give me a hug, it was like she made everything since the day I was born better. She gave her hugs unstintingly. If she didn't hug people physically, she hugged and embraced them emotionally, on the phone, anywhere. She let people know they were important to her.

I guess I am just in the beginning stages of being a real caregiver. I feel it with all my heart, and I know it is something I want to continue doing. Maybe I am not really good at it yet. Maybe I have a lot to learn. But this is the way I want to go.

To my dying day, being part of these women's lives will be a moment, so to speak, in my life that has enriched me beyond words. The people in that group will always be a gift to me.

"You eventually have to come to believe in something."

— Leonard, housekeeping staff member

LEONARD

The Hope to Believe in Something

When my aunt in England passed away of cancer, I was there only for her funeral. It wasn't until later that I realized it wasn't her I was crying for: It was myself I was crying for.

I was scared of myself. I was full of fear. Full of resentment. Full of self-pity. I am sure many cancer patients go through what I have been through. They resent that they have cancer.

At one time life was pure hell. I couldn't cope. I have never been in jail or anything, but that's what it felt like. Jail is just the way you lock yourself up and throw away the key. That's a penitentiary. That's the worst form of penitentiary.

I lost my dad when I was thirteen. My mom had to go to work. She was a teacher. My aunt was like a second mom. She was always there anytime I needed her. I could relate to her. I could tell her exactly what was bothering me. I could tell my mom, too, only mom had to be the breadwinner, so most of the time there was nobody at home. When my aunt was gone, in that final sense, my world was shattered. Something very important had been taken from me. Ironically, her death was almost a gift. It was like the whole bottom dropped out, and I didn't know how to cope with it. I started to go to Alcoholics Anonymous. It was AA that helped me deal with the realities of life.

The first step of AA is very simple. It says that I am powerless over alcohol and my life has become unmanageable. I deal with the unmanageability of my life on a daily basis. Every day is a new day for me. It is the unmanageability of one's life that leads people like myself to the bottle. Once I came to deal with the realities of life, then I came to accept whatever life has to offer — whether it be death or a sickness in the family or working around patients. I am grateful for what I've received, and at the same time I've got to go out and serve the next person. I give a lot, but I receive even greater.

I feel most comfortable around people who are ill. I can relate to them. I feel at one time I was a sick fellow, in a different way. I want to offer my friendly nature every day. That's how I am able to cope with my aunt's passing away of spinal cancer. Yesterday is dead and gone. There is nothing I can do about yesterday. I can only learn from my mistakes of yesterday. Tomorrow is not here yet, so what am I doing worrying about it? I worry about just today.

If you told me, "Len, here's a house, here's a Mercedes, and here's a hundred thousand dollars, take one drink," I'd say, "No thanks. I've been to hell. Now I gotta' give. Now I gotta' give, no matter what." When I help somebody, it gives me that joy.

Someone took a chance on me giving me a job. I knew I wouldn't disappoint them. Basically, who do we let down? We only let ourselves down. I feel I've got a two-fold job. One of the folds is to keep the building clean, be courteous and polite to the staff and patients. The other side is to give to the patients. For that I've got to have a half-decent attitude. To work in a place like this, you've got to have dedication. You've got to have feeling. A lot of feeling. You know when you walk down these halls that facing cancer is really hard for some people. I think it's necessary that we as staff make the first move. That *I* make the first move. Just say, "Hello, how are you?" The first day some people might not say anything back. If you want to know how someone is feeling, you look at their eyes. That's how I know. Eventually they start talking to people like me. It's important not to expect them to laugh or smile at you. With the hurry and scurry of it all, maybe you're the only person they've seen all day. Maybe you're the only person they've said good morning to all day, besides the nurse and the doctor. I just try to get the best out of each person I meet.

For them to be happy, I've got to be happy. I can't possibly give anybody something I don't have. I just try to listen. That's a therapy in itself. Just let the person pour out everything. They tell me things they say they would never tell their doctor.

The kids get to me. At times I think, "God, I've had the good life. I'm sober. I've got the gift. I've got the gift of life. Why do you have to take these kids away?" I knew one little one who really got to me from the time she first came. She was only two or three weeks old. I watched her grow up. She was a real sweetheart. She was two-and-a-half years old when she passed away at home. She used to call me "Lenny." Man, it hurt when she died.

You eventually have to come to believe in something. If you cling to nothing, you're gonna' end up with nothing. If you want to believe in that lightbulb, go ahead and believe in the lightbulb. When the lightbulb goes out, you're gonna' be in trouble. I believe in God now. If you can't believe in God, believe in a group. A group is stronger than you are. You're just a single person. No one is an island. You've got to have a God of your own understanding.

I love working with cancer patients. They are fighters. They really fight for what they've got. They have become like a family for me. I have never gone home depressed. When I leave the hospital, the outside world depresses me. I see people feeling so sorry for themselves. These are normal, everyday, healthy human beings who are complaining about sweet nothing. Even some of my friends complain about sweet nothing.

Some people say this hospital is a general morgue. They won't come here. But, for me, it makes me grateful for what I've got: good health, a job, people who care. When I have that gratitude in my life, everything else is secondary.

"I only want to work with cancer patients if I can make a difference, and I can make a difference only if I do something to enhance the life of a patient."

— Lee, clinical coordinator of nutrition education and research

LEE

The Hope to Make a Difference

At the beginning, they didn't think I could do anything. One physician said, "You won't be here in three months." I can remember thinking, "I will last four months anyway!" There was an attitude of, "She's cute, we'll let her try." That was ten years ago. I'm not quite as cute anymore, but I'm a lot wiser!

The scientific question then was, "How can we nourish the cancer patient without nourishing the tumor?" We're not looking so much at that anymore. We now know more about what we are doing. We know which patients are likely to respond, which ones are likely to benefit, and to which ones we are really just offering false hope. We're looking at the whole person with more emphasis on the quality of life. That aspect appeals to me.

I have discovered another part of me — a part that has a tremendous need to be needed. I didn't know that about myself. When I talk to patients, I can get totally wrapped up. I can forget something that had upset me only an hour ago. I am a changed person. I am more aware of how insignificant a lot of things are. I don't get upset about trivialities like I used to. It's not worth it.

I'm calmer. I'm more sensitive now. People say, "You must get used to it. You must get hardened." I think it works exactly the opposite. I think I get incredibly sensitive to the point where it can be hard on me.

It is hardest when the young patients die. I recall a twenty-year-old man who was admitted right off a ski hill. I remember watching him slowly go down, losing pound after pound, which was devastating to him. His physical appearance had always been important to him. He was on yet another chemotherapy. He said to me, "I would let them hang me in the corner by my heels for three days if I thought it was going to cure this." That has always stuck with me. People are willing to go through anything to be cured. I think we forget this. I think sometimes we lose track of how desperate people are to be cured. I've come to understand that people have a tremendous sense of hope and courage.

There are other kinds of challenges. Jane was young. She treated me as an equal. She wouldn't let me have any defenses. I knew there were absolutely no walls. She wouldn't stand for it. I think I understood for the first time what it would be like to die at my age. She was able to put it into words.

I didn't want to socialize with her. I didn't want to go shopping with her. I never did go, and she called me on it more than once. I knew if I did, I would suffer when she died. I knew I couldn't invest that much. I had made the mistake of having patients as friends before. For me, it just doesn't work. It interferes with what I can do professionally. It doesn't mean that I don't care. It probably means that I care enough to be sensible. Each of us has to decide our own limits.

There are depressing aspects, and there are lots of day-to-day frustrations in my work, but not in the areas you might think. It's not the patients. I've come to learn that when a patient orders a fresh fruit plate and says, "I can't eat this crap," the crap they are talking about is a feeling and a sense of the whole situation, not the food.

Part of what is depressing is that people are still dying. They are still suffering. We haven't made major, major breakthroughs. I thought that by now we would have a better handle on the basic cause of cancer. We still seem to be guessing.

The other part of what is discouraging and frustrating is to justify and rejustify and rejustify our part of a diminishing budget. I am having trouble looking at budget cuts in the healthcare system as a challenge. I would hope that I can ride out the storm, and that when things settle down there will be reason to be optimistic. I want to re-establish programs that we have had to eliminate. If we can't do that, then I don't think they need me. I only want to work with cancer patients if I can make a difference, and I can make a difference only if I do something to enhance the life of a patient.

"I accept what I see. I don't ask many questions of people. I feel my task is to listen."

— Ida Mary, volunteer pastoral counselor

IDA MARY

The Hope to Withhold Judgment

I was born into a Catholic family in a rural area. In my growing up years I never went more than five or six miles away. Our only means of transportation was by horse and buggy or wagon. Somehow I always knew I would be a Sister. I never had any second thoughts. I knew nothing about them and had never seen one. But I always wanted to be one. That comes from God. I can't explain it any other way.

I entered the Community of Sisters of Providence when I was twenty. I hadn't finished high school. Eventually, I took teacher training and I taught for thirty years. I taught mostly in the rural areas. When I came into the city — where I had no way of knowing my students — I just got turned off.

I suppose I was ready for new challenges. I started volunteering at the Cancer Institute. There was a special kind of challenge there. It was impossible to meet everybody the same way; no two people have gone the same path. I found new ways of using my gifts.

I wasn't always a compassionate person. Working at the Institute as a volunteer has helped my compassion grow. My compassion has deepened. I used to feel people either have compassion or they don't. I realize now the more one uses it, the more it grows. If you never utilize it, never nourish it, it never grows.

I never go to the hospital without spending time in prayer asking God to use me as a channel of Divine compassion, blessing of peace, or healing. I feel then I go fortified. I then have nothing to fear. I come just as I am. I accept what I see.

I don't ask many questions of people. I feel my task is to listen. Just being with each person is important. Being present with someone is forgetting about my concerns, my anxieties, so I can hear what they are saying. Sometimes it takes a long time before I really know what's bugging someone. Patients take time to trust. They can see into a person. They have a lot of time to think when they are sick. They have time to reflect on each person who comes into their room. They can tell who really cares.

When I first started to visit people, I used to weep with them. Now I don't have tears in that way. I feel very deeply for them. I can get very attached to them. They become family members as I get to know them. When they die, it's very difficult for me. Sisters hurt too.

Being a "Sister" used to mean you had to restrict your feelings. We were almost a blueprint of one another. Today I am much freer with my feelings. I can get angry. Sometimes I lash out at God. When I was blind for a while, I was very angry. What does a Nun do with anger? I lived with it. Like anyone else I asked, "Why am I like this?" I said to myself, "I'm not the only one who is going through this, and I could be worse off."

Later, when I was a cancer patient, I had the experience of feeling like I was no longer in control. As a volunteer, I could do my own thing at my own pace. When I was a patient, lots of other people were controlling me. I know what it's like to be told, "You have cancer." Perhaps that's part of why I'm able to reach some people. Perhaps there is something extra we share.

The chats we have are not always spiritual. We talk about anything. God is in all of life. We talk about whatever their interests are. I do pray a lot with patients, but prayer is something that must never be forced on someone. It only makes people resentful. If it's someone I'm not sure wants prayer, I wouldn't dare open my mouth, but I can pray within myself.

When it comes to prayer or communion, if someone asks for it, who am I to judge? Who am I to say no? The Lord would never say no. One of my treasured memories is walking into a room where two women were both weeping. One asked if she could receive communion that morning. I said, "Certainly." She added, "We are both dying. We're both going to the same place. Can we be united here by communion?" I could never have said no. It was a special time I will never forget.

"It's a black hole not to care."

— Nola, nurse and nurse educator

NOLA

The Hope for Authentic Feelings

I have to admit my uncle's death really drew me up short. I think it caused me to sit back and ask, "What do I really want out of life? What is really important? Who is really important? What should I be doing?" The answers are still unfolding.

No one prepared me for the difference between a loss experienced as a nurse and a loss in my personal life. My patients touch me deeply, right to my soul, but their connection with me is short-lived. I hurt when things don't go well for them, but I have the satisfaction that my impact on their life is good. I almost feel I have no right to get annoyed at anything in my life because I can walk home, and I have my health and they don't. Nor do they have much hope for getting their strength back. The other way I work is to say, "This could be my sister, my brother, my grandmother." I personalize the whole situation. It gives me more energy to carry on and to do a good job.

When it is the nursing part of me, I seem to want to work harder. But when it is my own personal life, there is a lot of security, companionship, and friendship wrapped up in a personal loss. It is harder to say, "Right, I did the very best I could. I contributed to their well-being." My energy gets drained. My motivation gets sapped. I don't want to go out there and work harder.

When I lost my uncle, I lost a friend, a mentor, and a father. He was like home base. I always thought of him as wise. He was someone I always checked out my plans with. When I broached the subject of going into nursing with a number of people, they said, "You'll never make it. You don't have what it takes to be a nurse." When I heard that, I thought, "We'll see!" They thought I was too forthright in my approach and that

I lacked the caring that they would expect from a nurse. It was my uncle who said, "Well, there comes a time in people's lives when they have to do something different. Go for it." And I did. I hadn't been nursing long before I realized there was a part of me that was quite sensitive, that I could do a good job, and that I did care about people.

I kept the caring part hidden in my outside life. I maintained an aloofness. I suppose I was emulating my uncle. He was a very private and stoic person. No one asked him personal questions, at least not more than once. He liked to get off by himself in nature and think.

If I fell and bruised my knee, he would say, "Stand up, don't cry." So I would stand up and not cry. When someone you admire tells you not to cry, you don't. I didn't — for a long time. Like him, I valued my privacy.

Like him, I like to be alone. When I'm with people too much, I become tense. I have to have time for me. I don't experience loneliness when I'm alone. I experience loneliness when I'm in a crowd. I can handle the cocktail conversations, but most of the time I don't make small talk easily. Sometimes I have to talk to myself when I get in these situations. I tell myself I have to realize these people haven't seen what I have seen. They haven't just seen someone hemorrhaging to death, and I can't expect them to have a pensive, thoughtful attitude. Many of them have had no reason even to think about the deeper questions in life. Nothing has shaken them into asking, "What's it all about?"

My uncle's death caused me to sit down and ask, "What is going on here? Do I need this hectic life?" I felt a need to get in touch with myself and my inner feelings. To do that, I needed to think. For me to think, I have to go for long walks; I have to sit on my porch in my chair reading a book, stopping to reflect. I can't think if I am rushing around. Maybe some people can. I can't. I need nature to allow me to think. The times when I have tried to insulate myself from the pain and suffering, I have been worse than if I had allowed myself to feel it. Sometimes I go off after work and have a little cry in the river valley.

For me, there is a reverence for life. It means enjoying the sunshine, the rain, a dust storm, walking down the city street, and looking to see the pleasure, to smell the fresh air. It means bringing the country with me to the city. It's working hard in my garden. It's reading a good book. It's being with people I enjoy. It's even being with people I don't enjoy. It's learning to choose. It's learning I can't care for everyone. It's having an obligation not to cause pain in this life and to ease it when I can.

I know that I want to be less aloof, less judgmental. I want to be willing to be more vulnerable and more open. I want to be more willing to share. I am hoping to be more gentle.

I think I am willing to be as open as I am because of my faith. Without it, I wouldn't even know myself. I wouldn't know how to be open. I worked as a nurse before I had a faith in God and after. Before, I wasn't bothered by death. I could look after someone who was dying. I could stand in the room with a hurting family, but I didn't seem to have the feelings that went with it. I was concerned about that. I seemed to be quite willing to go in and help my classmates. Maybe I was even intrigued with the whole process, but I didn't feel anything. I wished I could. Some of my classmates would go off and cry, but I didn't.

The real transition in my life came when I became open to God. My technical care was no different, but what I noticed was that I didn't have to generate that inner caring anymore. I didn't have to *try* to find it. In addition to the technical, I now had the feelings, and they didn't cripple me as I was afraid they might. Instead, they gave me more strength, and I didn't have to manufacture feeling sorry for people. My sadness was authentic.

If you try to isolate against the feelings, you get hard. If you try not to be touched by the pain and suffering around you, you are not going to make it. It sounds contradictory. You have to be open to the pain and then you can deal with it. If you try to block it off, then you become cynical. It's a black hole not to care.

The
HOPE to
Heal

The Bereaved Family's Story

"Death ends a life . . . but it does not end a relationship,
which struggles on in the survivor's mind . . .
towards some resolution, which it never finds . . ."
R. Anderson
"I Never Sang for My Father"

If it was courage I saw in patients and commitment I admired in caregivers, it was pain I felt in the bereaved. The power of loss to leave an indelible mark on the survivor(s) is without question. The loss of a loved one challenges seemingly every dimension of our lives. It queries the past and threatens the future. It gives rise to inscrutable questions and less than satisfying answers. It defies us to ignore our own ultimate end and to pursue the interim with integrity in the absence of sureness.

The nature of the relationship to the deceased seems less important than the existence of the bond itself. Each type of bond simply invites a different meaning in its loss. Grief is a land of incomparables. No one's loss is the greater loss. It is not possible to compare the loss of a child to the loss of a parent or a partner.

The loss of a loved one brings us face to face with the puzzles of life that have plagued the most scholarly of minds. The irony of longevity is to bury those we love. The irony of love is its invitation to say hello to that which we must also inevitably say good-bye.

Knowing we do not control the ultimate outcome, we struggle with the fairness of the timing and the process. We bargain for more time and less suffering. The two are often incompatible, and we are left with the ambivalence of our compassion and our selfishness. To lose a loved one and not die with them may be more difficult than to die one's self. It seems the deepest of challenges.

The healing begins not with an awareness of hope but of pain and grief. Each bereaved family member who speaks in this section of the book expresses not the nature of their hope, but the nature of their wound. Few knew the nature of the resolution toward which they were moving. Each somehow knew they would survive. Each knew the first step was to move with and beyond the pain. The remarkableness was not in their pain but in their willingness to go on with their lives. Therein lies the hope.

"I can still see the flowers, but I don't feel them."
— Sabine

SABINE

The Hope to Feel Again

McFarlane's life was about service: service to his wife, his job, his friends, his daughter, his country. My whole life was McFarlane.

I wondered if God took McFarlane to teach me that Christ has to be first. For me, McFarlane was always first. One woman said that was a sin, but a Catholic Sister said, "Isn't that beautiful. God will love you for that because you saw God's love in McFarlane." In the home he grew up in there was no envy, there was no gossip. There was only kindness. There were ten children. They all loved each other. I saw all that in him.

He never talked about his belief in Christ. He lived it. People talk about religion; McFarlane never did. His faith was something personal for him. My husband tried to have direction in his life, to be like Christ, and that was his personal affair — to serve people.

With my husband I was always myself. I had great respect for McFarlane from the time that I met him. It was romantic from the first minute. From the very beginning I had an immense trust. I suddenly knew this was something quiet and deep. It was something I could never explain. I had a very quiet and wonderful feeling. Some people told me I was out of my mind, meeting this man only three times and then marrying him.

As long as we were together, little else really mattered. We always enjoyed things together. We were the romantic types. It's nice to sit across the table and look at somebody you love. It's something special. There is a moment of peace, and you don't have to run after anything. Now I feel like running all the time; I cannot find any peace. McFarlane used to say, "I love you more than yesterday, less than tomorrow."

It was a Tuesday when the doctor said, "He will be as good as new. Everything will be all right. He will be able to go home soon." Wednesday, my husband said, "Sabine, let's go for a walk." I thought there was something unusual about the way he said it. I asked, "McFarlane, it's not cancer, is it?" He said, "I am afraid it is, Sabine." I thought I would scream or cry or something. Not cancer!

We were completely unprepared for the doctor to say, "I'm sorry. It's too late. It's already gone to the bone." My husband asked, "What does that mean?" The doctor answered, "I will give you two to three years. It will be very painful, but don't worry: We have medicine that will help with the pain." That proved to be wrong. He suffered terribly. I suffered with him. I thought, "If I could only be lying there instead of him." Three more years! We had looked forward to McFarlane retiring and being together. We always said, "Together forever."

He was sixty-two. Sixty-five had always meant magic. Breakfast together, walking together, no running away. He wouldn't have to wave good-bye and see me at lunch. (He always picked a house or apartment close to work so he could come home at lunch.) We would have everything. We wouldn't have to worry about another thing. We thought like a child thinks. Isn't it silly? Life is not like this. But something in me is still like a child.

I didn't say a word to anyone. Neither did my husband. We didn't say anything, even to each other. We went to the park. I didn't have to ask. I knew what the diagnosis meant to him. He knew what it would mean to me. We were not people who would show our feelings much in public. We didn't have to talk about it. I knew what he would say before he said it. He used to say, "It's really frightening, Mrs. Mont, how you can read me."

As I went home that night, I looked at all the others on the bus and wondered what they had heard that day. Maybe there were more who had trouble. When I got home, I laid on the floor and stamped my feet and knocked all the kitchen cupboard doors back and forth. I thought, "Not cancer, after all this." It was something we had never counted on.

With this cancer, I knew it would be the end. There could only be two cancers: the cancer that drags on and the cancer that kills quickly.

This one wasn't fast. There were lots of terrible things. I had no help at home. We never knew you could get help.

I still have one of his suits. It was the one he wore the first time he went to the hospital and the one he wore the last time. It was a blue suit with a little ascot tie. One especially difficult day he looked at me, and we both thought, "What will it be?" He made his salute like a soldier. I knew that meant, "This is enough, now comes action. Whatever comes, I will take it as a soldier." And he did. He always said, "Thanks, Sabine, for your encouragement. I don't know what I would be without you. How would I face this?" I thought, "If he only knew how little I face it within."

It is worse now than it was right after his death. I was so numb. I stayed in bed sometimes. I thought I would die. That was my hope. I didn't. I thought, "Do I really love him so little that I can't die? Why can't I die?"

There's nothing to do but live with it. I am amazed how I can smile and do things without a heart. I can be among company and not be really there. I am not me. It's a strange thing. My mind can do anything, but my heart says, "Don't fool me." You do not know how many nights I lie in bed and cry, how I wake up every morning and have to face the day. I know lots of people go through the same thing. That doesn't make it any better for me. I feel for them. I do not say I am the only one who is suffering. I do not like to compare my sorrow with the sorrow of others. There are so many pains in this world. I never say, "I have more pain than you."

Pain comes from your heart. It doesn't stop, even if you say, "Now, be sensible," because it doesn't come from your brain. You're always alone. I'm much lonelier when I'm with others. It's then I see what it is that I am missing. Nobody understands. For a while I lied. It was an easy way out. McFarlane wouldn't have told a lie. At night I would think, "Oh my, my sins are growing by the dozens!"

I can still see the flowers, but I don't feel them. A friend said, "Don't you hear the birds sing? It's so joyous." It's not joyous to me. I see it. I hear it. But there's no feeling. Something has changed. I can't explain it. There is nothing. Ian, my grandson, said at Christmas, "It was very nice, but I miss Dada." He cried and he said, "I don't understand Jesus. He has Dada all the time. Why can't He send him once in a while to us?"

I wonder, too. I am not angry at God. But with everything that has happened, I just haven't found my way back to God yet.

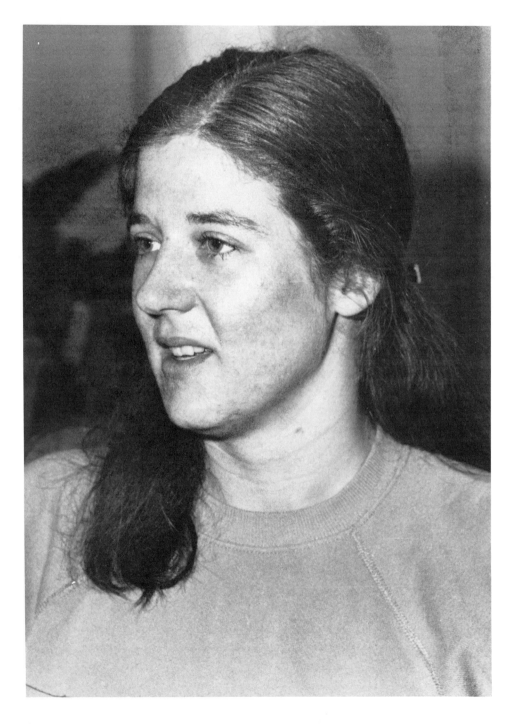

"*I get the sense of being an adolescent all over again. I have the same choices to make: Who am I? Why am I here?*"

— Kathy

KATHY

The Hope to Face Adulthood

It seems like all the changes in my life took place in a six-week period. My life was like that stupid Dickens' novel: "It was the best of times and the worst of times." I found out Mom was dying, then got engaged, then got married, then Mom died. It was bizarre. I was angry at her for dying and leaving me alone. I was angry and hurt for the grandchildren who would miss having a neat grandma — all those typical things.

She was very important to me. We were more than mother and daughter. We were best friends. I think a lot of people, including Mom, worried that we were too close, that she had too much influence on me. She was different from me, but I treasure those differences. She was flighty and disorganized. I am very organized and goal-oriented. She was highly creative and would have crazy but beautiful ideas. I tend to be more realistic and down to earth, so she was an inspiration in many ways. I was always proud of Mom. I admired her motivation. I was very fortunate to be her daughter because I learned the place of honesty and caring. She modeled that all the time. I feel grateful she lived as long as she did.

The big thing is that I don't have her in my head. I can't construct conversations with her, and I don't know why. Maybe she is still too much in my heart. I can feel her sometimes. When she was alive, I could talk to her about any problem in the world. There was never even the typical adolescent thing, "I wonder what my parents would say?" I would go home and I would ask. She was in many ways the archetypal mom to everybody in her life. What I miss most is her friendship. There are a lot of things since her death that I would like to talk to her about.

I get the sense of being an adolescent all over again. I have the same choices to make all over again. Who am I? Why am I here? What am I going to do with my life? I am at an existential questioning time. I am feeling like, "What is the purpose of being here?" My answer of late has been, "There is no purpose in being here." It's up to me to get my priorities back in order and to figure out who the new me is. No one else can do it for me. I am being impatient with myself. I want it to be over already.

I am changing from young adulthood to full adulthood. I'm starting to come to terms with the fact that life isn't exciting; that life is basically a matter of getting through. Hopefully, you enjoy it as much as you can, but there's no guarantee that your job's going to be rewarding, that your social life's going to be good, or that you are going to have the energy to do anything. I am going to have to deal with the maternal instincts I have been feeling. I don't know how much of that is to recapture the mother-daughter relationship, but the intellectual part of me is frightened. I don't know if I can be the type of mother I want to be.

It is important not to have a child because the lady next door has one and babies are cute. Maybe I worry because I have seen death, and I have seen how tenuous everything is and how bloody short life is. I am questioning the purpose of marriage and family. "Do I want to do this or not?" I don't have goals anymore. I am living a robot-like life without a whole lot of emotion, and I think I miss intensity. I miss those incredible highs, and sitting here crying today feels so good, like that stupid old song, "It's good just to be feeling." I think to a large extent I have shut down emotionally in order to survive. What I have done is to withdraw. At times I feel the responsibility of relationships is more than I can cope with. I can't give right now, and if I can't nurture people, I can't get nurtured.

There is not a single area of me or my life where I am pleased. I don't feel I am doing anything in my life well. Most of the time I feel I don't control my life, my life controls me. I am at the threshold and, if I am not really careful, I am going to screw my life up irreparably. I want control over my life. I think to a large extent I just feel burnt out. I just feel so damn old.

I truly believe healing is a function of time. I know what I have to work out: It's not just Mom's death; it's how I am feeling about life at the moment, the sense that I am at a cross roads. I am the type of person that has to solve all her problems by talking about them. I am aware that these problems are of the magnitude that I am going to need more than a chat over a couple of drinks or coffee.

I tried to go out and see more of my girlfriends; I tried writing in a journal. I tried simply getting more sleep; I tried living only for today. I tried positive affirmation statements. They really helped me get over being angry with my brothers. I took relaxation classes to help me unwind physically. I tried not working weekends. I tried variations of playing with my work schedule.

Maybe at some level I am running from something I need to face. It's partly coming to terms with my own mortality, which is natural when you've lost somebody. Mom died. The grey hairs have started, the wrinkles have started. Maybe at some level I am trying to come to terms with being an autonomous person even though I am in a marriage. I have a thousand roles in my life, but the most important role — being my mother's daughter — will never be again. Mom would give me a pep talk if she heard me talking like this. That's part of why I miss her. I still need those talks.

"I did the fear, Jessica did the rage. Bob did the hope, and Joseph did the living.
We all did the pain."

— Bob, Deb & Jessica

DEB, BOB & JESSICA

The Hope to Share the Pain

DEB

I can remember when Joseph was born: I got this strong urge to pray. I hadn't been into praying. I hadn't been a church-goer for many, many years, but I said a long prayer for this child.

As a new mother I didn't know how a mother should be. Only six weeks earlier I had been a professional woman. Joseph was a happy baby with the oddest laugh, and he was easy to care for. He was very engaging. Even as a baby he seemed to have a long attention span. He loved to play with his shadow in the doorway when he was in his jolly jumper. He was hard to get to sleep. My husband, Bob, made a cradle for him, and we would swing him until he drifted off.

It was near Christmas in 1984. Bob and I had taken my father to New York for medical treatment. He was in a coma and totally paralyzed by medication after bypass surgery, so there was already a major heartbreak in the family. Joseph and his grandfather had been close buddies.

We got a phone call. Joseph had a bad cough. No one was very concerned, and he was on cough medication. It was a shock to get another call saying that within twenty-four hours Joseph had gone from a trip to the doctor's to the specialist to the university hospital, two hundred kilometers away. It was Christmas day. We flew home immediately. They told us right from the start it was probably cancer. We nearly lost him in the biopsy. The next fifteen months that we had Joseph were a gift. We could have lost him that first day. Instead, it was a long fifteen months.

As a parent, you go through the same pain as your child. He had to have lumbar punctures and other painful procedures. We had to help him get through them. The only way I could do it was not to feel the pain I was having. If I had felt the pain, I couldn't have done it. He would balk the odd time but never really seriously. He let it be known that it was a drag. After a while we got so we could sense who among the medical staff knew what they were doing and who didn't. When they didn't, I felt like saying, "Look, go practice on an orange. Don't practice on my kid." The specialty teams were terrific, and they listened to Joseph.

Joseph died at home. I think I had been afraid of his dying, yet I recall this very strong presence. That is the only word for it — a very peaceful, loving presence. The morning before, Joseph wanted somebody to get him some fish, goldfish, so we got him some fish. Then he asked that we get everybody together — Mommy and Daddy, Grandma, and Uncle Blair. I asked about his sister, Jessica, but he said, "No, Jessica is too hard." Then he said, "Now, Mommy, you know what to do." I said, "Joseph, I don't know what to do." He insisted I knew what to do. I asked, "Joseph, do you want me to pray?" "Yes, Mommy, that's what I want you to do." So we prayed in a circle around his bed. We all told him how much we loved him, and he seemed to settle after that. Later on he said, "Come on, guys, it's time to go! Is everybody ready? It's time to go." It was as if he was talking about what was beyond. It was like he could see through somehow.

When Joseph was alive, I knew what to do. I had to help Joseph get better. I had an important function, a purpose in life. When he died, I had a feeling of not being needed. There was a sense of intense emptiness and lack of direction. My life was no longer directed from the outside, and it was hard to find internal direction. For me to get a sense of direction again, I had to experience all the pain I hadn't let myself feel, all the anger and all the sadness.

The whole experience strained our marriage. We were juggling school and work. We would see each other in passing. Bob would have breakfast with Joseph at the hospital. We didn't have much of a life together. When Joseph died, we were both exhausted. It didn't help that I had to have emergency surgery the next week. Poor Bob, he was wondering if he was going to be surrounded by illness and death forever.

We had very little to give each other, and I had unfair expectations. I felt that if I felt empty, Bob should feel empty and that somehow he should be able to make it go away. I had to say to myself many times, "Wait a minute. If I feel empty, that's me. It is not Bob's job to feel it. Or if I feel scared, it is not his job to make me feel not scared. It's my job. It doesn't mean he isn't there. It's just that it isn't his job to be the Band-Aid."

It was as if by losing my son, I lost my relationships, and I lost the illusions about myself. One by one they slowly slipped away. It was frightening. I felt like a child again. I felt like I did when I was five years old and wanted someone to show me how God worked.

The one thing Joseph's death taught me was there's a life after death. I know now that death is not the worst thing that can happen. That makes it possible somehow never to stop caring.

We never really told Joseph that he could die of cancer. Whatever he knew, he stayed unafraid throughout the experience. It seemed like I did the fear for him. Jessica did the rage. Bob did the hope, and Joseph did the living. We all did the pain!

BOB

I had really wanted this baby. I used to talk to him all the time when he was still in Deb's tummy. It was our job to help Joseph grow and to help Joseph live. We didn't think it would be our job to help him die. How do you help a son die when he is only seven?

The process of helping Joseph gave Deb greater satisfaction than it did me. She would sit with Joseph at the hospital, and she would feel like she was where she was supposed to be, doing what she was supposed to be doing. I didn't. We tried really, really hard for Joseph, but it seemed each of us had to do our caring alone. We were more like a tag team. Maybe if we had been in a community where we were known, it could have been different.

We were thankful that Joseph wasn't any younger because he could understand that the "torture" was part of the treatment. He understood that no one was deliberately hurting him. I can remember one night he had a lumbar puncture. It was painful for Joseph and for me. I can recall thinking that they were going to bring in the next child, and then the next one, and that the medical staff would have to do that day after day, child after child. I wondered how they did it.

I was looking for anything that anyone could tell me that I could interpret positively. I always worked on the assumption that Joseph would make it. Deb was never convinced. I am glad that I didn't have to know in advance, and see in advance, that there would be an empty chair at the table. It wouldn't have helped. All the way through, one thing we didn't want was to meet a parent who had lost a child. We didn't want to be confronted with the *fait accompli*.

The relapses were hard. The first time Joseph was in remission made everything up to that point seem like a bad dream. We thought we might have it beat. The first relapse was the hardest. I can remember hoping he wouldn't die and crying because I was so afraid. It was just so sad.

It seemed like Joseph didn't want to talk about his illness. He would get very impatient. It was of no interest to him. He just got frustrated with us, as if to say, "Lay off it." He seemed to have a gift of tremendous inner peace. No matter what life threw at him, he hardly ever got rattled and never for long. He took things in his stride. He just accepted it as normal. It was just what was happening. Certainly nothing he ever said suggested that he thought this was out of the ordinary. He never seemed to ask, "Why me?"

I can remember the night Joseph died. I had been praying it would be over. I realized that there was only one way out for Joseph, and that way was dying. Trying to keep him alive was no longer the way to help him. I could tell he was in no pain. There was no tension in his body. I told him I loved him and he told me, too. It was time for his morphine shot. By the time I started to walk out of the room to get the medication, he was gone. Just as he died, it started to snow.

I know Joseph is all right. It is not like my child was abducted and is perhaps suffering all kinds of terrible things. I know what happened. I was there. He was there. The people who were really important were with him, and I know he's all right and that he doesn't need anything more from me.

One of the most wonderful things about the way Joseph died was that we were there, very close to Joseph. There was no withdrawal from Joseph.

After he died, I felt like the whole world didn't work anymore. There was almost a paradoxical reflex reaction in that I withdrew from Deb.

Deb and I are different. Deb wants to understand. I take the engineer's approach: I just want it to work. I don't aspire to understand. My tendency is to be like a porcupine: to curl up in a ball and create distance between myself and the world when I suffer.

At some level I feel a sense of failure and loss. We put everything into trying to keep Joseph alive, and it didn't work. There didn't seem to be any room for us. Then we had to start picking up the pieces of our lives.

For us, the lifeboat approach wasn't the answer. We weren't going to hold onto each other and hope we could beat off all the sharks. We knew our relationship couldn't be based on fear. We had been individually shaken at a deep level, and we were exhausted. It is really hard to be supportive when you don't have anything to give, and it is frustrating to be expected to be supportive. The crack in our marriage started to show.

Suppose you have a piece of wood, and it has the odd little crack in it that you don't see. If you bend it over something, putting as much stress on it as you can, the cracks start to open up. That's what was happening to our marriage. Under the circumstances we were in, we had to prioritize where we put our limited time and energy, and our relationship never made the list. What made the list was going to the hospital, the logistics of living and just surviving.

I think you have to work things through as individuals, but at the same time you have to be committed to the relationship. If the commitment isn't there, the relationship won't be there when you're through. After Joseph died I had to look at everything again. Some of my values got reconfirmed, but it was like I had to look under every rock. For me, the only alternative was denial, and I knew that wouldn't work. To deny Joseph died was to deny Joseph lived. I am not prepared to say good-bye to Joseph in that way.

I am working my way through a lot of things, and I expect to be different than I was before. I sense now that I could lose everybody. I nearly lost Deb a week after Joseph. I don't take anybody for granted. I'm not sure how to deal with that. Do I deal with it by putting as much as I can into the relationships I do have? Or do I cut my losses by withdrawing and having relatively little to lose?

JESSICA

I think hospitals are special places. They have to take care of peoples, and the nurses and the doctors never have to sleep there.

I can remember when Joseph died. He was wrapped in a blanket. I know when someone is not alive 'cause I have seen statues. He died a long time ago.

Mommies cry more than daddies 'cause that's the way God made them. God is a special person. That's who Joseph is with now. He's in heaven. It's a sad place 'cause you miss your family. When I am sad, Mommy helps, and it helps if you put your finger in your mouth. It helps you stop crying.

If I thought Joseph could hear me, I would tell him all sorts of stuff. God and Joseph talk about things. I think God has to tell Joseph things, but I don't know what. Only God would know.

"When you're sad, it helps if you put your finger in your mouth."
—Jessica

"It happened for us, it can happen for someone else."

— Liz & Art

LIZ & ART

The Hope for a New Life

LIZ

What stands out is how much Don suffered and how tired I got. I watched him go from working heavy construction to sitting in a wheelchair in two months. He survived ten months after that. That was a long ten months. I got so tired. I am still tired. I can't seem to get over it.

We couldn't plan ahead or do anything. We never knew from one day to the next. I don't know how many phone calls I got telling me that he wasn't going to make the night. Three days later he would have recovered enough to come home. It was like a rollercoaster. I got to the point where I would wonder whether it was worth going in to the hospital when they called. I always did, but it wasn't easy. We lived fifty miles out, and I didn't drive.

Don was on medication every two hours. I was going twenty-two or twenty-three hours a day without regular sleep. I would stay at the hospital in his room seven or eight days at a time. The staff was tremendous. They would come and relieve me so I could go for a cup of tea or a shower. Those little things counted so much.

When he was dying, I couldn't go in the room. I tried going in once, but he was pleading with the doctor, "Help me. Help me," and I couldn't take it. I knew he was at the point where nobody could help anymore. Some people judged me. They thought I should have been there the last few minutes. They didn't see me there the previous nine months.

While Don was ill, the worst part was I felt so divided. I felt I should be with him, and I felt I should be with the kids. He felt I should be with him all the time, but Dawn Louise was fifteen, David was eleven, and Danny was just four. I never was much of a disciplinarian, and I was even less so when Don was sick. After Don died, I seemed to be trying to buy them everything they wanted to make up for something. Maybe I was just too tired to give them what they really needed. I was just exhausted.

I was used to being alone, with Don having worked away so much, so it wasn't the aloneness that got me. I'm not sure what it was. I lost fifty-two pounds in three months. I developed a food phobia. For a while all I ate was a bowl of Special K a day. I went through a bad period where I couldn't even decide what to wear in the morning. I would get so frustrated that I'd just throw my clothes at the bottom of the closet. I guess it was stress. When I started getting a severe pain in my temple, they wanted me to see a psychologist or psychiatrist. I couldn't afford $75 an hour.

The turning point was when I went to a bereavement group. That's where I learned to cry. And that's where I met Art. I ended up starting a completely new life.

ART

I was twenty when I was married. I never claimed to be the best guy, but I never cheated on Madeline and I always held a job. I've never drawn an unemployment check in my life, and I've never been on welfare. Mind you, there were some months that were skimpy. After being married for twenty-five years, I was lost by myself. Even with my kids I didn't feel right. I would visit one. I would visit the other. I would stay at one place and then stay at the other's. I didn't feel like I had a home anymore. I drove a lot. I would take the poodle, go down to Calgary, have coffee, and turn around and come back. Drive to Red Deer. Have coffee, turn around, and come back. Go to Barrhead, any place. How can you be everywhere and nowhere? I was very lonely. I suppose frustrated, too, almost peeved that after so many years Madeline could die. It was as if she had just up and taken off. Her death was only part of the problem. Four other people important to me died in less than a year. I kept all the feelings bottled up.

For some reason my friends didn't ask me questions. I felt like an outcast. I think it happens to everybody. Your friends still talk to you, but your partner is missing. You don't fit. You make a threesome, not a foursome. They don't pass you on the sidewalk without talking, but there's never an invitation like there used to be.

I talked more than once about getting rid of myself. I probably didn't have the guts to do it. I knew I needed a professional to open to. I knew I couldn't open up to friends in the same way. As for the kids, I figured they had enough on their shoulders. After I got up the courage to go for help, I found it easier and easier. I never looked back. I started getting a sense of what I wanted in life again.

I wish I had started talking earlier. When Madeline was dying, she and I both knew it, but we feared talking to a professional. I suppose we thought they would give us the low down on when she was going to die or how we were supposed to go about doing this. Ever since I was born, I have had to do things on my own. I thought I had to grieve this alone, too. It was two years after Madeline died that I met Liz, and that was a hell of a long two years. I met Liz in the grief group.

With the group we were all in the same boat, so it was a lot easier to talk about problems. It took a long time for me to get started, even to get there in the first place. Once I got there, I felt confident that what I said at the group would stay in there. If I talked to a friend, they could, without meaning any harm, tell another friend who might tell another friend. It would be like a story: Pretty soon it would get exaggerated.

Liz and I go back to the group sometimes. It gives them hope. It lets others know that there is light, that there is hope, that they shouldn't keep everything bottled up. You can't heal until you make some room for it.

We have our own business now. We are into a regular routine. It happened for us, it can happen for someone else. It hasn't been easy, but it has actually been beautiful for us.

"Nobody talked. It was incredibly lonely. My grandchildren are the only ones who freely talk about him."
— Mary

MARY

The Hope to Break the Silence

He walked in the front door at four o'clock in the afternoon on a Thursday. It was my day off. He said, "I have cancer, I'm dying." He started to cry, and the first thing I did was scream and say, "Why are you doing this to me?" He just asked me to hold him, and he cried.

We'd had five kids and many a battle over the years. There was a lot of hurt. Ted gave his all to everybody else. It was an open-door policy and everyone adored him. He ate, lived, and breathed his work. He was a workaholic. He did a super job. I won't take that away from him. He only had a grade ten education. I was working full time. He had his life. I had mine.

I have read that a husband and wife can become much closer during an illness. There were lots of discussions I would have liked to have had but didn't. We rarely talked. When he took sick, we never talked about it. Nobody talked. Everyone avoided the topic of cancer and more so the subject of dying. It was as if people were afraid that they were going to catch it. I was literally stunned. Everybody knew that he was sick. He didn't want the kids to know. I told the kids. Everybody knew that he was dying, yet nobody said anything. Nobody said anything.

He was angry, very angry and frustrated. "Why me?" he used to scream and shout. There was a lot of feeling of powerlessness. He figured right from diagnosis, this was it! They told him that it was terminal. He felt there was nothing he could do. His anger was his way of venting. I was the only one, to my knowledge, that he let see his anger. I probably would have been the same way if I had been in his shoes.

My family was a loving family. I used to laugh. My dad was a Welshman, so when he cried, we had a good cry. With Ted, there was none of that. Ted would walk down the street and would question why I took his hand. He wasn't able to let that emotional side of himself out.

When I lost my dad, of course I cried. Ted gave me supreme "you know what" because I cried.

I could cope with Ted's illness, his anger, but not with his crying. I'd never seen Ted cry, never. He didn't cry when his parents passed away, when his brother passed away, his sister, his sister-in-law. He just didn't cry. I found his crying harder to cope with because I had never seen him cry before.

Within the week the cancer was spreading, and they operated on his groin. He shut down. We did it day by day. It was the way we had lived for forty years. I felt that my duty was with him. I was never sorry I was there for him during that period of time. I mean, I was with him for forty some years.

After Ted died, it was incredibly lonely. I walked out of that church alone. Everyone else was paired up. Nobody took my hand or put their arm around me. They were all involved with each other. His immediate family was right behind me, and nobody leaned over and patted me on the shoulder. It's funny. They put me right at the front, so I walked down the stairs and past the casket alone. It was all I could do not to break down. I didn't want to because I knew Ted wouldn't approve. At the cemetery I finally turned around and said, "I need to get out of here." I was halfway up that hill when my son-in-law came over and put my coat over my shoulders. I have had this feeling of being alone ever since that day. When they threw the dirt in that hole, it was like they threw five hundred people with it. I didn't see anybody after the funeral. I don't know what a widow is supposed to feel like, other than lonely. I don't have a sense of a shrouded black widowhood that is supposed to go with this. I had some practice living on my own, but I miss the companionship. It is like a painful endearment.

I think I built a wall around myself. I had been hurt too many times. My mom was sick for nine years. I lost my parents and I was heartbroken. I still miss my dad. I lost Ted. There is a soft spot still there, though. I've got my family and that's what counts.

I adore my grandchildren. I can be quite free with them, and I just love them. They don't judge feelings. The biggest sense of joy is watching the little ones grow, their little triumphs. For a while they didn't talk about Grampa, but then I started talking about him. It upsets me if they don't talk about him. My grandchildren are the only ones who talk freely about him.

"I now know that only I can make me whole again."
— Val

VAL

The Hope to Be Whole Again

"Val, what's leukemia?" "Domenic," I answered, "it's cancer." It was like pulling the plug out of his very existence. He was sure he was going to die. That's when I got my goat up. He couldn't give up on us. I wouldn't let him. I wasn't letting him die and it was that simple. I said, "You can do whatever you want, but I'm not losing you, Buddy Boy, you're not going to die!" That kind of set the course.

I don't know what he felt the first day at the hospital. He was a very private person. I only know what I felt: a total vacuum. I was scared. I went upstairs to the ward with Domenic. I looked out the window. It seemed like the coldest, emptiest room I'd ever walked into in my whole entire life. I didn't know how to go about doing anything at that point, I was so floored. I was just picking up Domenic and putting the pieces back together as best I could. I knew he was scared. He was shaking. We held hands.

That evening I went to the lounge. It was homey. The head nurse could see me with tears running down my face. She asked, "Do you need to talk?" and I said, "Yeah, I need to know more about leukemia." I wanted to know what it was, how it worked, what happens with it. The thing that impressed me was that I could feel her pain for me. I cried for a while. For the first time through all this, I cried in front of someone else.

Domenic needed a reason to keep on. I was pregnant. That was his biggest reason. That was the major thing that kept him going. It is important for Italians to have a son to carry on the namesake. We got a son and Domenic was "out of his mind!"

At points I was so torn. My husband was all-encompassing and important to me. He was going to be gone forever. My children, on the other hand, were little. They needed me, yet I knew that in time they wouldn't remember and that they would go on. How do you decide where to be when you have little kids who are screaming and a husband who is dying? I decided, "I have to be with Domenic for me, not for him. I can't feel guilty when he dies." The kids hated me for leaving them after they had fallen asleep. I learned to leave them before they went to bed. They could accept that.

When he was home, it was just he and I after the kids were asleep. A whole new side of Domenic came through. My husband, my partner, and my friend came through. That's what I miss most now. It didn't matter if we were playing cards or doing puzzles, having incredible tickle fights or rolling on the floor horsing around. We didn't go out much. We didn't have the money. We'd just sit and be quiet and be close. We had the feeling that everything was full. It was a sense of warmth and caring and sharing a total oneness. We didn't need to say anything. When Domenic died, he knew what was most important to him. He knew how he stood with his family. I'm so glad that the last words he ever said to me were, "I love you."

I'm at peace in my own mind that I did everything that I could for Domenic. I was there twenty-four hours a day. I took care of everything that I possibly could. When he died, I had nothing left. I was zapped right out. I was like a waste land.

The only reason I had for living after he died was the kids. I soon realized I was the one holding it all together. I started to realize that if I wasn't happy, if I wasn't content, if I didn't have the things I needed for me, this wasn't going to work. So now I'm starting to give myself a break. I'm doing things for myself. I'm finally doing my hair, putting on my make-up, taking my shower every day. I'm back into trying to feel like a human being again. I know I can't be superwoman, and I don't expect it of myself anymore. I'm human, I'm tired, and I can't be strong anymore.

At first, I needed to run. Whereas the kids hurt some of the time, I hurt most of the time. In a hospital you can't run. You have to sit there. But after the death, you can get out. As long as you can face the fact that you need to run, it seems to get better. I still need space for me. I need to get out. I need to be myself. Even when I came home after Domenic had died, I wouldn't let anyone give me sympathy. It was something I couldn't handle. "Don't show me sympathy, I've got to keep it together." I wouldn't let people kiss me, touch me, hug me, nothing. I pushed everyone away. I needed that space and control over the one thing I could control: myself.

I hardly ever cried in front of anyone all through this. If I don't want to cry in front of you, I won't cry in front of you. It's as simple as that. I'm a very private person, too. Not just anyone is going to see my pain. That is mine.

Before I met Domenic, I felt that a part of myself was missing. When I was with him, I felt whole. He gave me something I didn't give myself. A part of me died when Domenic died. A part of who I had become was gone, and I had to accept it was gone. I had to find that part again. I now know that only I can make me whole again; only I can make me be happy, satisfied, content. I have grown. I can look forward to each new day and its challenges again. Who I am hasn't changed that much; I just accept myself more.

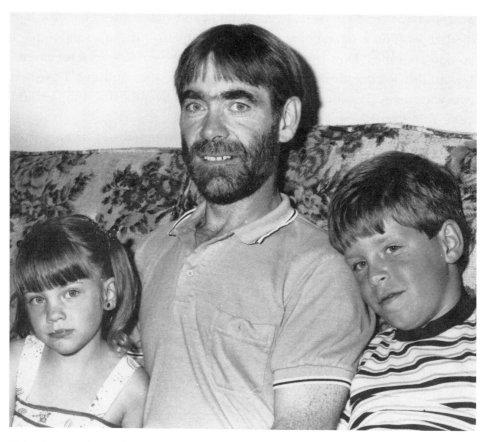

"I had to reach out for something."

— Dennis

DENNIS

The Hope to Reach Out

It was all happening at a time in my life when I didn't know where I was going. I was questioning the routine of everyday things. I was wondering, "Is this all there is?" It's like you get to the top of the mountain. You reach it. Now what? I was working through that, and then my wife gets terminally ill.

I met Val in the fall of my second year of teaching. Everything was calculated in our marriage. There were no debts. The only debt we ever had was the mortgage. We had everything figured out. We had the weekends and summer holidays for five years before the kids came along. There was no real pressure.

When they finally told us the cancer was progressive and incurable, it was on Jennifer's third birthday. Val cried for a while and then I cried. I wondered, "How will I do this? How can I raise the kids?" It was very selfish. It was a kind of panic.

People get numb about death. It's not real. It just can't happen; it only happens in the news, not to us. We're too young. Val gave a hint at one time that she might die, but somehow little things just didn't sink in. It was the toughest, toughest thing to realize. We just went day by day. We took it as it came. In June the cancer was progressing rapidly. No one asked, "How long?" There were hints that maybe things were bad. The Tuesday night before she died, it hit me. I was numb. I was like a robot. They told me, "She's dying," and I couldn't believe it. I wasn't prepared for it. All of a sudden, there was "something." I just wanted to reach out to her. All of a sudden I wasn't worried about my responsibilities. I was looking at her. I had to give all that I could. I held her and stroked her face and wished I had more days like that to share with her. It's frustrating that we didn't have more time to talk.

I don't remember a lot of things. They say shock lasts a little while, but I don't agree. It can last a long time. I eventually gained calmness, and numbness took over. I don't know how long it lasted. It became so bad I saw a psychiatrist. He put me on medication, and then I was numb again. Eventually I figured, "Hey, I've got to do something, I can't run away." It took me a long time to get to that point, but I'm there now.

After Val was gone, I realized what she contributed to my life. There's a void that will never go away. I realize that the kids are there; but for a while I didn't think I could raise them by myself. Society and people around me implied that a single father can't do the job; he needs help. I almost convinced myself it would be better if I was gone. I was that close a few times! I had sleeping pills. It hurt so bloody much that Val was gone. She was so much a part of my life. When I went past a favorite place to bike, all of a sudden I wished I could play some of this all over again. There were so many good times. It could have been even better.

Sometimes I took things for granted. I didn't realize how important they were. The world frustrates people so much. Work gets more hectic as time goes on. We give so much to everything else that we have little to give to each other. We get tired, we don't always communicate. Val kept a lot of things inside of her, too. She didn't want to burden me with little problems. The little things that should have been important, we didn't always talk about. I wished now that we could have shared them. Little things don't seem important, but they make a relationship even better.

At first I was desperate to go out and meet someone; to fill a void or hope that I could kill the pain. Everyone has a void in their life whether they're married or not. Just by grabbing someone to fill up an empty place doesn't mean everything is going to be okay. It is not that easy. I had to make sure I was secure in my own way.

Our society is really cruel. There is no backup. We're like a race going no place. I don't believe in praying for magic. I don't look for miracles. I don't pray for miracles, just for the strength to get through the day and to be good to my kids.

My main purpose in life now is to raise my kids well. Jennifer wasn't even three when Val got sick. Jennifer was very close to her mother. The screaming she did for a while was just traumatic. Geoffrey is a very quiet boy. He was very worked up inside, but he wouldn't say anything. He detached himself. Once I came home a little late, and they were both in tears.

You don't know what goes on inside a kid, but they're hurting. Jennifer has to have flowers on the table. She is trying to be the lady of the house. Mother's Day is tough on both of them. Jennifer made a card and gave it to my sister. Geoffrey made a card for Mom and just brought it home. He doesn't want to be singled out.

I had outside help for a while. After that, I did it on my own. I was going to get a nanny, but for some reason it didn't work out. It wasn't meant to be. I do all the housework myself. I find it relaxing in some way. Val would be proud of me. My weekends are so thrilling. I go grocery shopping, pick up the kids, do the laundry. I've accepted it, though. I realize that self-pity doesn't help. I do it and I don't think about it. You have to forget about the fact that you're hurting. You have to realize that you've got to go on. You've got a purpose.

I couldn't believe that people could hurt this bad when somebody dies. A line in a book I read has stayed with me: "Life is difficult and you have to suck it up and blow sometimes." A lot of people can't understand that. They think, "How can you stand being in the house by yourself?" I can. For a while I thought, "How can I survive?" But I would do a little bit of this and a little bit of that, and eventually it would be time to go to bed.

Death changes things. My whole religion collapsed. People used to say, "It's God's will." That was the hardest thing. I almost took those sympathy cards and chucked them. Everything I thought I knew or believed completely collapsed; I had to build my religion from the foundation. I read the Bible. I tried to build on that. I wanted to believe so bad, but belief doesn't come by intellectualizing. It has to come from the heart. I had to reach out for something. I have days when I wonder if I want this faith, but it is the only thing that gives me hope. Val's death affected the way I look at other people. I try to give more. Val gave so much love, and maybe I wasn't giving enough in return.

One of the things Val has done is to take the fear out of dying for me. Dying's not so scary anymore. It makes the promise of life after death much more precious. I have that hope and faith. I realize that eventually I will die. There have been times I wished it would happen soon.

Some people say the pain goes away, but I look at it different. You learn to handle the pain. You learn to accept. As grief goes by, it's like Val is more present. I can sense her more. She's somehow there. It's a little leap of joy. Sometimes there's a little bit of lifting inside. The pain is still there, though. I'm empty. I still have a hollow feeling.

"I've been helped by the little things that I have done for other people."
—John

JOHN

The Hope to Pass on the Caring

We had been married seventeen years. Marilyn was a beautiful person, a very determined person in a soft-spoken and quiet way. When she spoke, everyone listened. She was very caring and very strong. Neither of us had had any major illness to deal with before her diagnosis.

The cancer was detected fairly early. Marilyn wasn't sure whether she wanted a mastectomy. That was a big question. She had a few days to think about it seriously. We didn't tell each other what we thought. We agreed that at five o'clock on the second day we would let each other know how we felt. When the time came, we both agreed that there was not much choice. A woman from the Mastectomy Visiting Program came over and talked with her. A well-dressed, impressive lady walked into the room, introduced herself, and made Marilyn feel a lot more reassured that the operation wouldn't be as devastating as she had anticipated.

Marilyn used to make a very valid point that nothing focuses your attention like the word "cancer." We did a lot of reading. From the time she was diagnosed I would go to the library and get everything I could to read about cancer. The most difficult thing was that everything was of a highly technical nature, so it was hard for an average person like me to understand what was going on.

We thought things had gone so well. When she had finished the follow-up radiation treatment, she was invited to give a speech at her old sorority for a special occasion. When she got ready, she was more beautiful than ever. We joked that she was still beautiful, but it just took her a little longer to get that way.

It was a great disappointment when the cancer reoccurred. Marilyn had always thought of chemotherapy as the worst possible thing. We met with the oncologists who told us the pros and cons of radiation versus chemotherapy. Chemotherapy won out. There was no way of knowing if it was the best choice.

I'm not sure at what point we were aware that Marilyn's chances were not good. I suppose it was when she went on chemotherapy. We were never told that she had reached a stage at which she was going to die. To this day, I feel that we should have been informed more about the progression of the cancer so we could have been better prepared.

Marilyn got very ill on the chemotherapy. The most horrifying thing for her was that she started to lose her hair. She had beautiful hair and cared for it always. For the twenty-one years that I knew her, she never once had scraggly hair. It was almost like she started giving up on the idea of recovery when she lost her hair. We got two very good wigs, and most of her friends never knew that the hair was not her own.

Marilyn used to say, "You know, it's easier for me than it is for you because it's my cancer and not yours. Everybody expects me to be sick, no one expects you to be tired." At times I was exhausted, but I kept going because there was no alternative. I didn't realize how tired I was getting. I did strange things. I would be very tired, and yet I would go home from the hospital and sit up reading until three in the morning.

People talk about cancer patients being "victims." Think of what the word "victim" brings to mind for people. Once Marilyn was diagnosed as having cancer, people talked to her in a different way. Instead of saying, "Hello, how are you?" it was, "Hello, how ARE you?" I found people would say that same thing to me after Marilyn passed away.

I felt some people resented the fact that I wasn't completely devastated and my whole life hadn't fallen apart. If I said I was fine, I felt some people resented it, as if I was too hardhearted and wasn't grieving enough.

Initially, there are just so many things to do after one's loved one dies. My family and Marilyn's family were excellent. They provided a great deal of support. By this time I was behind in my work, so I went back to the grind quickly. I just never felt that Marilyn would want me to do anything differently.

The most difficult part is missing the type of communication that happens when you really know someone. It isn't just sitting down and having a two-hour discussion that I miss, because I can have that with my colleagues. It's knowing that there is somebody there who understands and cares.

I think of the times when Marilyn and I should have enjoyed things more at that moment. Since Marilyn's death, I am more oriented to the present. I seem to be less concerned with the long range goals and more concerned with the quality of my day-to-day existence.

I have developed a very independent life style since her death. I have found that I can communicate at different levels with different people on different occasions, and I think I've gotten satisfaction out of that. I quite enjoy my independence. I find that I can live a very independent existence, and it doesn't have to be lonely or meaningless. I became involved in volunteer work. Throughout our experience we felt so fortunate to be near the hospital. I would see patients and families arrive on a bus and then spend hours waiting. I resolved that was something I could help with later. And I did. I became very involved in the Cancer Society.

In the personal domain, I think being a male and being raised to hide feelings has made it more difficult to come to grips with how I feel and to really allow myself to grieve. I have found it helpful to talk with other males who have lost their wives. Some have had even greater difficulty than what I've had because they've not been raised to share their feelings.

I've found that by helping other people I'm helping myself. I've been helped by the little things that I have done for other people, and that's more important for my adjustment that I am willing to admit. There's a saying: "The fragrance of the rose lingers on the hand of the giver."

"There is a continuity. My wife had been dead for more than a year, but here was this new life."

— Reuben

REUBEN

The Hope for Continuity

My granddaughter's name is Dina Rachel. Dina is Hebrew for Donna. I was married to her grandmother, Donna, for twenty-nine years. We had five children — a boy and four girls.

Donna's first mammogram was negative. She was told to come back in the fall but given no specific date. I have never been able to understand why she delayed when the lump was getting larger. Five months later, the second mammogram was positive. At that stage I was upset, but it just didn't occur to me that her condition was all that serious. The doctors treated her with radiation and chemotherapy and never spoke about the cancer having metastasized. Her regular checkups were uneventful.

The seriousness set in when the second tumor was discovered about a year later by her family doctor during a routine checkup. Previously, the doctors kept talking about "hot spots," but they never really explained those words to me. I expected her to have a mastectomy. When I said something to the doctor who performed the biopsy, his answer was, "What good is that going to do?" I must have looked puzzled. He said, "If you don't understand what I have told you, phone me." When I look back, I must have been a real idiot because, in effect, he was telling me the cancer had metastasized and I was afraid to ask. After hormone treatment, with some apparent initial success, Donna's condition worsened.

She had to give up driving. She couldn't go grocery shopping. There wasn't very much that she could do around the house. She had been working, and it was an awful blow when her boss told her, "We no longer need your services." Gradually, as she had more and more things taken away from her, her quality of life became minimal. Her physical and emotional pain took a heavy toll.

I was trying to understand what was happening to Donna, not paying a great deal of attention to what was happening to me and the rest of the family. I remember on a number of occasions sitting down with her and asking her to talk, and she wouldn't do it. I let her set the standard as to how much we talked about things. I suspect she had some apprehension that, because of my past medical history, I might suffer another heart attack.

At age forty-two I had had a serious heart attack. I was lucky to survive. I really don't think I could have pulled through without her support. Yet when the situation was reversed and I realized how serious her condition was, I was unable to support her. I could never talk to her because I didn't know how to talk to her. It wasn't only me. Some of our long-standing friends didn't know what to say or how to say it either.

Nobody said at the outset, "There is more to this illness than just the physical aspect. You may as well know that, and there is help for you." It still disturbs me that I only learned in the later stages of her illness that there were psychological support services available from the outset.

I recall going to see the doctor in the early stages because I was worried about the emotional impact on the family. He gave no direction and said, "You have to learn to live with it." It was a friend who told me how to get help. But it was so late in the process. Precious time had been lost. By the time we availed ourselves of the services, a lot of irreparable damage had been done.

I feel I was deprived of the opportunity to say good-bye in a meaningful way. A month before Donna's death, I made an appointment to see the doctor. I put it to him bluntly. I asked, "What is the situation?" If it was "terminal," and I used that term, I wanted to know. He assured me, as he put it, that they "had not reached the bottom of the barrel yet."

When Donna was admitted to hospital for the last time, she did say, "Over the next few days we have a few things to talk about." She didn't say anything more. I knew she meant only the two of us, so I didn't probe at that time. Suddenly and unexpectedly she took a turn for the worse. I had hoped that she would rally and that we would be able to talk. That never happened. She died within an hour.

After Donna's death I could not overcome the sense of having lost the opportunity to console my wife. If I would have been able to talk to her, maybe she would have explained certain things to me. In Donna's case, not only was I cheated, but I felt she was cheated.

I was angry, not only with the system but also with myself because I felt like I had missed the boat. I hadn't been as probing as I should have been. I should have insisted on being told, so at least I could have had options as to what I could have done. I felt that I had let Donna and the family down.

I am a lawyer. I think logically. This was something I couldn't deal with logically. It's totally illogical and totally bizarre. No matter how much training I had, there was no way I could sit down and attack the problem using any methods I had been trained with.

I didn't realize there is a real grieving period. For some people it's short and for some people it's long. In my situation I feel the grieving was extended because I was left in a situation I couldn't accept. I wanted to scream. I did make an appointment to see the doctor. I wanted to impress upon him the emotional damage that had been done. I'm not sure, though, that anything will be different for the next family.

I suppose I wanted a quick fix, but there was no way I was going to get it. The initial emotional damage was something I could not overcome at that point. It had to run its course. I had to stay alive through it. That was a difficult choice. There were times when I didn't want to live. I just felt there was nothing for me. It took many months of extensive therapy to get me out of the abyss. There was no doubt about it . . . I was at the bottom. I don't make any apologies for my behavior.

I was emotionally exhausted by the time Donna died. I had nothing left to fight with or for. I tried to carry on what people would consider a "normal" life after, but there is no "normal" life. It could never be "normal" again. The fact is that my wife died at an early age, at a point when she had a lot to live for. She wanted to live to experience the joy of a grandchild.

Donna's death was shattering. There are so many things I took for granted — so many things that Donna had done. Suddenly, I was left alone. There isn't a day that something is said or something is done that doesn't remind me of the past. As time has gone, at least I can sit down and talk about what happened without breaking down in tears.

I knew I had to purge myself and get the grief out of my system. However, I found out that I can't get it all out of my system. Part of it stays there like a numbness. The injury is still there; I just don't feel it so acutely.

There's a scar that will remain forever. I realize that what happened to me unfortunately has happened to many other people. Yet that doesn't make it right. I should have had a choice. I could have been made aware of the truth about Donna's condition without breaking any confidentiality pact the doctor had with Donna, if indeed there had been one. It shouldn't have happened the way it did, and time doesn't heal that deep emotional wound. I have to accept what happened and try to make the best of it.

The most healing aspect for me was to be present within eight hours of my granddaughter's birth. It was thrilling. I was able to hold Dina and to realize that there is a continuity. My wife had been dead for more than a year, but here was this new life. Dina is not a substitute. Dina is a continuation.

II.

Reflections on Hope

Enabled by Hope

Like the people whose stories are recorded here, all of us, sooner or later, are participants in hardship. Whether our lives are touched by illness, accident, poverty, or injustice, hope is part of our life's journey. Thankfully, hope is seemingly as much a condition of life as suffering. The experience of hope is somehow "enabling." It helps us say, "I can" — maybe not today, maybe not perfectly, maybe not without fear, but "I can. I will at least try." What is puzzling is that no one is quite sure how hope "enables." What is this phenomena that is considered essential to survival — that moves us forward, often against unknown and untenable odds? Why consider hope at all?

The importance of hope is recognized in the writings of scholars and professionals of various bents. Theologians, philosophers, psychologists, and healthcare professionals all concur that hope is crucial to their work and needs to be the subject of investigation. Yet it is surprising that there has been a virtual scientific neglect of so consequential a human phenomena. Only recently has the scholarly world begun to turn its eyes in the direction of hope.

Much of the medical world has more concern for "false hope" than curiosity about spontaneous remissions. It is not uncommon to hear the expression "hopeless case," as if survival is only a matter of statistical probabilities, as if survival is the only object of hope. Nursing, which accepts the mandate of instilling, restoring, and fostering hope, is far from being able to substantiate its claim that nurses are able to influence hope levels. Only a few prominent philosophers have ever approached the topic directly. Theologians cannot agree about the nature of hope. And the helping professions flounder in their efforts to "fix" people's hope. It seems much is as yet unknown about this ill-defined and little-researched aid to recovery and adjustment. What do we know about hope?

Hope is a complex, difficult-to-articulate-and-measure intangible. We have no agreed-upon definition of it. It is a relative to courage and trust, an antidote to fear and despair. It has been considered both a curse and blessing. It has been the subject of storytellers and minstrels, of poems, of music, and of myths. Whether we are experiencing difficulty or we are attempting to help ease the suffering of someone we care about, we seek to enhance hope. We somehow sense it is enabling.

There are problems with hope! The challenge of every helper — family, friend, or professional — is to encourage hope that is helpful. The challenge of every patient is to use whoever and whatever enhances a sense of hope. Professionals are not the sole dispensers of hope. Each of us has the potential to help or inhibit hope, including and perhaps most importantly, the patient. The problem arises when helpers and patients differ on what they believe is helpful. What one person may see as potential, another may see as nonsense. What one may perceive as the "reality" of the situation, another may experience as a pessimistic view. I am reminded of a patient who accompanied me to speak to a group of medical students. Jack told them bluntly, "You can tell me the odds, but don't tell me when I am going to die. Only God can do that!" What is "realistic"? Whose "reality" shall be honored? These are important questions, not just about prognosis, but about the many day-to-day "realities" of living with illness.

I wish I could say that I have never met a caregiver — professional or otherwise — who was intentionally unhelpful. I cannot. I can say, however, that with very, very few exceptions, people want to be helpful. They want to enhance hope. If they are inept at it, it is rare that their intent is to hurt. Being hurtful and unhelpful is more often a matter of caregivers presuming their view of "reality" is somehow endowed with greater truth than that of the patient's.

As caregivers, we face many — but different — questions than patients:

> "He seems so down — what should I do?"
> "She is so scared — what should I say?"

"Is he denying?"
"Is she pretending just for us?"
"Should I encourage her to take the chemotherapy?"
"Is it silly to talk about going on a trip, knowing we probably can never go?"
"Can we handle things at home?"

These are questions of hope. There are no pat answers. I will, however, attempt to share what I have come to understand about hope from my work and from my reading. Like the stories shared in the first section, "Experiences of Hope," these "Reflections on Hope" are intended to further your understanding of hope. Unlike the stories, the focus will be more on thoughts about hope than personal experiences of hope, more on a thinking than a feeling level. As you read, perhaps you will be prompted to think more about hope and to be more "enabled" to provide the kind of hope you want to give to those you care about — including yourself. Toward that end, I invite you to reflect with me on these four questions:

• What is hope?
• When is hope helpful?
• How is hope related to who we are?
• What can we do to enhance hope?

What Is Hope?

There are many questions to be asked about the nature of hope. Where does it come from? What is it? Can it be shared? How is it different from other related experiences? How necessary is it to life? How do we know if a person has it? How do we enhance it?

Clinical observation informs us that some people die long before their projected prognosis, and others survive far past theirs. Those people who refuse to die "on schedule" are often viewed with interest, but prior to fifteen years ago they were seldom investigated. Unexplained recoveries were simply called "spontaneous remissions," and long-term survivors were labeled "real fighters."

One does not have to be a professional to realize hope is important in getting well physically and emotionally. Supposedly, people in the helping professions are in the business of hope, and their training has emphasized the link between hope and the ability to adapt and find meaning in difficult situations. However, parts of their training can actually mitigate against acceptance of the "intangibles."

Yet intangibles set the stage for medicine. The best medicine and best caregivers are powerless to restore health in the absence of hope. Regardless of prognosis, chronic illnesses are fear-inducing for many people. If fear gets the upper hand, hope diminishes. *Hope is a crucial antidote to fear.*

Although hope is an intangible, it is still important to make efforts to include it when helping someone. However, hope is not given with a pill or a needle. Hope cannot be seen on an x-ray. No food contains it. No blood tests can detect it. It does not magically come back as a function of physiotherapy. Hope is given and received through human relationships. If you are involved in a patient's illness experience, the patient looks to you for hope.

This is especially true if you work in a healthcare field. Because of the authority often ascribed to professionals, you are in a powerful position to enhance or diminish hope. You become an important person in the patient's life, whether you want to be or not. Interaction with the patient is itself a treatment. Inherent in your interactions is the potential to do harm or to enhance healing. The question for all who are caring for someone who is ill — professionals included — is not whether or not to have a relationship with the patient, but what will the nature of the relationship be? Many factors affect the kind of relationship we develop with people who are ill.

Our life situations influence hope. The level of physical functioning we have, the roles we play in life, the relationships we care about, the families we live in, the limits of our financial resources — all these factors affect our hope. Our experiences and concepts unite to produce a hoping process, the goal of which is to deal with the uncertainty in life — to ward off fear and despair.

Hope is most commonly found in a context or life situation that has an element of captivity or, minimally, uncertainty. Stories are told of the physicians imprisoned in concentration camps, risking death in order to secretly assemble a crude x-ray machine to assist their rudimentary medical practice in those austere circumstances. Uncertainty and a sense of being held captive are common among the ill or injured. Not surprising, under such circumstances time becomes important.

Hope is always set in the context of time. It draws on the past, is experienced in the present, and is aimed at the future. It is not always logical. Logical, "realistic" hope is based on information known in the present — most often, a statistical probability of something happening in the future. Hope, however, is more than a calculation of probabilities.

Hope is as likely to be experienced in the symbolic, unconscious realm as in the cognitive, rational realm. To the degree that this is true, a person can continue to hope against remarkable odds. This "not logical" aspect of hope is the aspect that is often the most difficult to understand and accept. This is especially true for professionals whose training has emphasized logic and science, who see the source of hope in technology, and who recognize the only goal of hope as cure.

Hope is experienced in relationship to someone or something. We draw hope from a variety of sources. Hope may lie in a purpose, a goal, a person, a procedure, a theological belief, our families. The nature of our relationships influences our choice of hope targets. Targets of hope can be concrete or abstract, explicit or implied, serious or trivial. I recall one young mother whose hope was totally invested, not in the pursuit of cure, but specifically in living long enough to ensure her son would have a mom to go with him to his first day of kindergarten. (By the way, she did.) Another person may hope to "die with dignity." Yet another may say nothing, while unrelentingly pushing themselves in physiotherapy. The object or target of hope provides a person with a benchmark by which to evaluate progress. Difficulties arise when there are substantial differences between what the patient and the caregivers regard as an appropriate target of hope. When the patient is insisting on returning to work and the physician is recommending making out a will, there is a problem!

There seem to be at least two levels of hope. First, there is the very specific hope that is more like a goal or a desire. You can recognize this kind of hope because it fits into the sentence, "I hope for . . ." Then there is a more general, and yet personal, kind of hope that is more difficult to describe. In writings about hope it is called "the hoping self." It is an intangible you can feel when you relate to someone. There is a sense of hope that is somehow present in the person or in the situation. This hope helps convey that the future is somehow benevolent. There is a "sense of the possible."

The experience of hope runs through all dimensions of life. Physically, people with hope report a greater sense of energy. (That is not to say that they are physically stronger, although they may be.) Their mood will be more up than down. This may mean they feel more confident and, therefore, ask more questions not always welcome by some professionals. Passivity and compliance, although valued for the absence of hassle, are not necessarily indicators that the patient is doing well. Optimism and realism are characteristics of hopeful persons. We tend to say people with these characteristics are coping well.

Hoping and coping, according to some theorists, are considered different but concurrent processes. Both assist in the management of the uncertainty inherent in an uncertain situation.[1] Both support each other. People who cope, but hope little, are "flat." They have lost touch with a sense of aliveness. They are more in need of hope enhancement than advice about how to cope. People who hope, but cope poorly, lack the ability to transform hope into action.

It is common that the hopeful person is action-oriented, i.e., planning, organizing, making decisions, seeking help. The action a person chooses is often dependent on being able to imagine that those efforts have the potential to be successful. For people who believe in miracles, the potential for remarkable or unexpected results is always present. Initially, action is targeted at cure, or beating the odds. Later, action might be more rewarded if directed to alternative goals. Again, not everyone involved necessarily reaches the same perspective at the same time. Sometimes it is the patient who is the first to realize that the target of hope needs to be shifted, and they expend energy convincing the doctor and family that they are ready to stop active treatment.

Hope is basically a shared experience. When people share hopes, the illness experience is less lonely, for everyone. It is difficult to hope alone. However, it is not necessary that the "other" be physically present. Hopeful people are somehow connected with other people and things that they care about. They are bonded to and care about others. Some may be staying alive for children or parents. Others, especially the elderly or people who live alone, may stay alive because they are concerned about a pet. To the degree that we understand the relationships people have with their world and the people in it, we are able to understand when and what kinds of hope will be helpful.

When Is Hope Helpful?

The question of the value of hope is a long-standing one. Karl Menninger points out that hope has been described by the Greeks as an evil, an illusion, the food of exiles, but that Martin Luther believed everything done in the world is done by hope.[2]

Part of the difficulty of accepting the value of hope has been, until recently, the difficulty of proving its value. In a world that values the quantitative paradigm, hope is often reduced to a set of predictable odds. In other words, many believe that it is necessary to demonstrate that the attitude of hope makes a difference in statistically measurable ways before we can conclude that hope is helpful. This controversy is close to being put to rest. The work of the School of Medicine at UCLA is well known for its interest and contribution to this debate. The whole field of psychoneuroimmunology is reflecting this new curiosity about the mind/body interaction. Many professional journals are readily accepting articles of a scientific nature with this bent. A lay person's summary of this work has been published by the respected Norman Cousins in his book *Head First: The Biology of Hope*, in which he indicates:

> There was abundant medical research to show that the brain, under circumstances of negative emotions — hate, fear, panic, rage, despair, depression, exasperation, frustration — could produce powerful changes in the body's chemistry, even set the stage for intensified illness. But there was no comparable evidence to show that the positive emotions — purpose, determination, love, hope, faith, will to live, festivity — could also affect biological states.[3]

Traditionally, "flight or fight" responses have been considered the standard responses to stress. It is now hypothesized that hoping is a useful alternative response. Hoping, however, goes well beyond wishing or desiring.

Behavioral medicine, psychiatry, and psychology have in the past two decades been addressing the issue of hope by developing a technology of hope, a plethora of strategies intended to "enable." These have included medical hypnosis, humor, biofeedback, behavior modification, goal-setting strategies, individual counseling, and group and family therapies. The effectiveness of these approaches is strongly dependent on the practitioner. These strategies often take time and a particular skill. Frequently, people in healthcare professions do not have the opportunity to train for or to use the technologies of hope. They can, however, convey the potential for a positive outcome about interventions to which they may refer their patients. I notice a considerable difference in patients' openness to treatment depending on whether the referral has been suggested as another possibility that may help, or as a last ditch effort that will also end in futility. Theorists, researchers, and practitioners need to recognize that positive expectations play an important part in outcome, and that the lack of hope can be a serious obstacle.

Given the evidence of the last decade, it becomes important for each of us to decide where we stand with regard to hope. How will we handle the patient, family member, or friend who "hopes against hope?" How will we approach the person who has given up? How will we keep our own hope throughout the years?

How Is Hope Related to Who We Are?

In order to understand hope, we each have to ask ourselves, "What are my own beliefs about hope? Where do I stand in my attitudes toward handling serious illness? Which beliefs will I translate into action?"

Commonly held beliefs about dealing with serious conditions

Alternative interpretations of commonly held beliefs

1. Denial is bad! Patients who express hope disproportionate to survival statistics are being "unrealistic" and need to be corrected until they are in line with the medical stance.

1. Some denial may help, at least for a period of time, particularly if a patient continues to do what is medically recommended. Denying the eventual outcome is not necessarily bad; recent research actually suggests that some denial may allow people to cope better.

2. When talking with people about serious situations, it is important to remain emotionally detached.

2. Patients look to others for a feeling of security and a source of hope. But, as caregivers, we need to balance objectivity with caring. Having some objectivity enables us to effectively analyze and more clearly make decisions about what needs to happen. However, the patient's feelings need to be considered in those decisions.

3. Patients must be told "the truth."

3. Anyone who is important to the patient is in a position to influence what the patient accepts as "truth." "Truth," in the medical world, is often discussed in terms of statistics. If patients believe "the odds" to be "truth," they tend to comply by dying "on time." The word of anyone in authority is very powerful. "Truth," in the patient's world, is often gathered from the experiences of others who have had to face similar circumstances. For example, people with cancer may look to other people who have survived cancer as "authorities." The helpfulness and subsequent hope that recovered cancer patients can give to newly diagnosed patients comes from an authority that is claimed by virtue of having been through the experience themselves.

4. Professionals know best.

4. The medical team usually has more knowledge about the disease and its management than the patient. Not uncommonly, however, the patient may have lived with a disease longer than the medical team has treated it. The patient and patient's family also know the personality issues that will enter into treatment and adjustment. They are the experts on themselves. Until the information that the doctor has is combined with the information that the patient and family have, the "best" is not known.

How would you respond?

The following situations are presented as opportunities for reflection as you further consider the issue of hope. Briefly let yourself reflect on how you would translate your present views into practice in these situations. Put yourself in different shoes: Imagine what your response would be if you were a physician, a friend, a lover, a colleague. How would your relationship to the patient affect your answers?

1. John has liver cancer. He is already egg-yolk yellow. He asks you what you think of visualization. What would your response be?

2. Mary needs open heart surgery. She is convinced that she will die from the surgery. She has had two dreams indicating this. Interestingly, her daughter has also had a dream of the same nature. Mary's heart condition is serious. What would your response to Mary be?

3. Trevor is diagnosed with testicular cancer. His wedding is set for three months hence. He asks you, "Do you think it is fair for me to marry?" How would you answer him?

4. Harold has just told you that he has taken out a million dollars worth of life insurance and feels good that his family will be well taken care of. He has a long history of multiple sclerosis. What would your response be?

5. Albert and his wife are both not strong. He has a heart condition and she has severe arthritis. They have been married forty-three years. They are people of considerable means. Their children want them to move out of their home. Their resistance is causing considerable family difficulties. What would your response to them be?

6. Louise moved to the country after her second divorce. She is socially isolated in a rural community with few resources. She is angry and afraid as she becomes aware of the realities of her severe diabetes. How would you respond to her?

7. Dorothy's life has been interrupted with serious ulcerative colitis. At this point, it is not known if her
   temporary colostomy will be reversible. At seventeen she says she wants to be a pediatrician. Her
   parents don't know whether to encourage her. They
   are also concerned about her very strong interest in
   mountain climbing. They have asked your advice.
   How would you respond?

Developing a frame of reference

Your relationship with a person who is ill can have a profound influence
on that person's hope. WHO you are is what you offer a person in need.
You can use your "self" to engender hope and confidence. If you want to
be helpful, you will need to develop ways of thinking that include some
of the following aspects:

- *Being open rather than closed:*
  This means allowing for alternatives. If you are a
  family member or friend who is skeptical that what
  the patient is hoping for can never happen, being
  open may mean saying, "I don't know how that could
  happen for you, but I sure hope it does." If you are a
  healthcare professional, being open especially ap-
  plies to the way in which you present information to
  the patient: You can present options, not a single,
  foregone conclusion.

- *Emphasizing potential rather than limitations:*
  This does not mean ignoring the limits; it means
  emphasizing the potential once limits are understood.
  Once the limits of medicine have been declared, it
  does not mean that the limits of human potential have
  been announced. You can help the patient to be open
  to new targets of hope, to draw on strength not yet
  experienced.
       I recall a retired gentleman who was challenged
  to adjust to a tumor that left him paraplegic. He was
  an avid golfer; he was also concerned that his wife

had never driven. One morning when I came in, he announced, "I've turned a corner. I'm going to find another hobby, and I'm going to teach my wife to drive."

• *Recognizing the symbolic and intangible, as well as the concrete and visible:*
We now know that, by practicing in our minds, it is possible to increase the likelihood of accomplishing something. Athletes commonly use these techniques. Consider asking the patient to imagine/picture outcomes that are helpful. Professionals trained in these methods can help people select and practice effective imaging. Having actual, tangible symbols and images in the environment can help, too. As caregivers, we can help by understanding which symbols the ill person finds hope-enhancing.

It is important, however, to recognize that a symbol which might be helpful for one person may not be helpful for another. For example, a religious person may find a cross on the wall helpful. But I can recall an agnostic woman who was disturbed by having to constantly glare at what, for her, was a symbol of confusion.

• *Being person-centered rather than role-centered:*
This involves coming to terms personally with such issues as ego, powerlessness, and the limits of caregiving. This will challenge you to examine your own capacity for empathy: How much can you identify with another person without being overcome with what the person is going through? Being person-centered means being a friend — dropping the masks of whatever other roles you may have.

I am reminded of one patient who was moved to intensive care at another hospital. She pleaded with me to help her get transferred back to our hospital. When I inquired as to her reasoning, she replied, "Because a nurse there cried with me." Sometimes patients need someone who accepts and cares and feels, more than they need someone who gives advice. It is not always necessary to be "the father," "the older sister," "the doctor," or "the social worker."

- *Being a partner rather than an expert:*
  Part of the difficulty of being a caregiver is the belief that "I am responsible": "I am the one doing the 'caring.'" "The patient is helpless." It is important to remember that patients have not become children who can no longer think for themselves because they are ill. They may need your help, but short of comas, they seldom need you to run their lives. To be a partner means conveying respect for the patient, seeing the patient as capable in all but unusual circumstances of having the capacity to make decisions about his/her own body and life. The most difficult test of this is when the patient chooses other than what the physician recommends. Medical personnel may be particularly vulnerable to succumbing to the "expert" role. Ultimately, however, in order to make good decisions, the patient needs to be well-informed but free from pressure.

To arrive at new attitudes and perspectives requires some reflection. In some ways this is the realm of philosophy. Whereas the scientist goes into the laboratory, the philosopher goes into the world of ideas. Originally, philosophers were not just philosophers; they were also the mathematicians, the scientists, the theologians. Interestingly, it was originally the philosophers of a society who were the healers, the shamans.

Socrates said, "The unexamined life is not worth living." Yet, a contemplation of the important questions in existence may lead us to give up philosophical inquiry and to accept the commandment of Ignorance: "Think not, lest Thou be confused." David Suzuki, world renowned scientist and environmentalist, has encouraged us to broaden our understanding of science and life with his quote of Charles Birch: "There's something mental . . . in life, which we let slip through our fingers in the past. From protons to people, you have to look at them more as subjects than objects."[4] To see people as subjects means to see them as people — not statistics, not unfeeling objects that are counted and researched. It is difficult enough to be ill. It is even harder to be treated like a thing.

If we are to have an open attitude, it means accepting that everything is filtered through our own experiences and beliefs, our particular view of the situation. Facts are not as objective as they seem on first appearances. Usually "facts" related to illness are based on averages. How factual or accurate they turn out to be in individual situations depends on many, and often personal or subjective, factors. If facts were facts, they would affect everyone similarly. For some, particularly those trained in the presumably "hard sciences," this is a difficult idea to grasp. "You mean, evidence is not evidence? Truth is negotiable?" Or at least, "truth is different from person to person?" You got it!

The important point is that each of us knows the world through our experience of it. Patients, physicians, caretakers, family, and friends have a vast stock of experience that may be different from each other's. The challenge comes when experiences vary and someone has the need to impose his or her conclusions on the other.

The sum of our experience is our story. Organizing our experience so it can be told as a story or narrative is our most common way of remembering what has happened in our lives. Stories enable us to connect parts of our experience throughout the dimension of time. That is, stories have a beginning, a middle, and an end. You may or may not agree with a patient who says, "I know this started when I lost my job," but that is the point in time when the story begins for that person. How each of us remembers and tells our story is unique. Each of us has a personal language of hurt, a personal language of triumph. Hearing a person's story is important. To the degree that people feel you hear and accept their story or reality, they will be willing to let you become a positive part of their story. In an effort to be heard by her caregivers, one patient wrote the following open letter to her caregivers:

Just because you understand my disease, doesn't mean you understand me. To understand I am ill does not mean that you understand how I experience my illness. I am unique. I think and feel and behave in a combination that is unique to me. You do not understand me because you have a label for my disease or because some distant relative of yours died of it. It is not my disease or treatment that you need to understand. It is me. This could happen to you.

And don't tell me you understand. Even if you had the same disease, you could not fully understand. I am tired of being told to:
- "Deal with your feelings" . . . by those who flee from any intimacy with me and cringe when I confront them.
- "Get your life in order" . . . by those whose lives are obviously cluttered with the unimportant.
- "Accept your pain and loss and even face death" . . . by those who avoid the very topic.
- "Live with your limits" . . . by those who move about freely.
- "Live life to the fullest in the time that you have" . . . by those who shield their reactions from any form of intensity.
- "Accept dependence" . . . by those who have the resources to assert rigid safe ways of being.

Don't tell me about how much you care, when you:
- are never on time.
- don't visit.
- assume I don't mind being touched.
- leave my bedside table out of my reach.
- imply I can't decide if I want to eat or not.
- imply I'm not trying because the treatment isn't working.
- discount ideas or questions that I have.

Don't tell me about hope:
- until you have heard my pain.
- until you are willing to be present for me.
- until you can stop judging me.

It is one thing to tell me there are side effects to chemo; it is another to know my fear when I am puking up my guts and my hair is falling in my soup.

What Can We Do to Enhance Hope?

Communicate care

It is impossible to speak of hope without speaking of caring. They are both important intangibles. A good deal is known about the communication of caring. "Core conditions" of caring are considered to include: empathy, unconditional acceptance, warmth, concreteness, authenticity, and immediacy. These are what Alice (see page 57) is talking about in her story when she refers to "real connections": "A real connection happens almost without words ... the real connection happens at the heart level."

Disclosing and sharing some parts of our own lives is involved in forming a real connection. Patients need to feel they are in a real relationship — one where they give as well as receive. If "professionals" are unwilling to answer at least some personal questions, it is unlikely the necessary trust will happen. When a patient asks, "Do you have family?" they are not prying. It is a way of inquiring whether you are in a position to understand their feelings.

Caring does not necessarily take extra time. You can convey caring by your tone of voice, touch and eye contact, as much as by words. Apart from whether a condition will respond to treatment, the conveyance of caring in and of itself is a treatment. It helps people in sustaining a sense of worth and, in so doing, increases the likelihood that they will approach maturely whatever adjustments are required or mandatory.

Hear the narrative

Not only do we, as humans, give meaning to our experience by "storying" our lives, but we are also empowered to "perform" our stories through our knowledge of them.[5]

It was Reuben (see page 141) who taught me the value of the story. In our first talk it was three hours before I asked only one question. During that time I had many feelings, not all compassionate. Somehow, though, I was able to hear his painful story. When he finished, I asked, "Do you feel anything is different because you have come today?" Tears flowed down his calm face, his eyes looked directly back to mine, and he said, "No one ever listened to my story before. I needed someone to know." I accepted his gift; I learned, "Listen to the story — the whole story." Patients often feel no one has been willing to hear more than snapshots of their story.

If a person is hesitant to tell you their story, or if your time is short, you can invite them to use some of the following techniques:

- write or draw in a journal. (Offer to read it at a later date.)
- write letters to a person of their choosing, explaining what has happened.
- make a tape recording of their story, first in "documentary length," then just the "highlights."
- draw a map of how they got here.

Caregivers need to have their stories heard, too. Professionals, family, and friends need a place to share their stories — a specific place. As Nola describes in her story (see page 93), it is difficult to make a transition from watching someone hemorrhaging to death to making "small talk." You cannot expect someone at a party to feel what you feel after being close to illness and death all day.

Make something happen

When you can make something noticeable happen quickly, you can open a person to the potential that the situation can be influenced. Phoning the physician and arranging for relief of a symptom, sneaking a pet in for a visit, providing child care for a few hours, serving the person's car, taking them to treatments — these are all small, but important, evidences that you can be helpful and that you care.

Professional caregivers can promote hope by such simple things as returning phone calls and being on time. Patients are discouraged quickly when they feel powerless to influence the very people who care for them. Patients who have to wait for pain medication begin to develop anxiety that their pain will not be controlled. Making a difference in symptoms makes an important difference for patients.

Share hope stories

"Hope stories" are simply stories about hope. You may tell them. The patient may tell them. You might ask the patient to generate one a day. Anyone among those who care can start generating them. You can put them on audio or video tape; listen for them in every piece of music and every television show. They can be concrete and specific or general and metaphorical. They abound in everyday life.

I remember a hope story I once came across in a magazine I picked up on a long flight. There was an article about a young woman who was facing a bone marrow transplant for leukemia. Despite her condition, she and her fiancé proceeded with their marriage. Her transplant was a success and their courage rewarded. Not all hope stories have perfect endings, but this one did.

Practice hope rituals

What are the rituals that the patient performs each day or week? How can they be used to enhance hope? What is done routinely and perhaps ritualistically that could be therapeutic? Hope rituals can relate to behaviors or to beliefs. One common hope ritual is the leaving of notes on the bathroom mirror as reminders to think constructively throughout the day. As people do their morning brushing, they repeat the posted positive thoughts over and over. Another common example is the notes or posters that kids love to make for the refrigerator door. Every time the door gets opened, the hopeful message is seen. I recall one family's hope ritual in particular. Despite their dad's advancing lung cancer, they regularly attended the Friday night fights so they could yell and remind themselves that, in some games of life, you have to fight in order to win.

It is also important to practice the ritual of respect. It, too, is crucial to the partnership of patient and caregiver. In Diane's story (see page 65), she describes the mistake of making assumptions about what a patient might want. She reminds us of the necessity of requesting, without fail, permission to invade the patient's body or space.

Encourage hope images

Images of an anticipated state or outcome can help a patient focus energies in a constructive direction. Not all patients have an active imagination. However, it is not necessary that patients be able to see in their mind's eye clear images of the hoped-for condition. They can simply have a sense of what a situation would be like. Remember, though, the ability to imagine can be developed and enhanced. If patients have difficulty generating hope images, recalling movies where something similar occurred, looking at photographs of someone in the anticipated context, or listening to "up" music that stimulates pictures in their mind can help.

Music can be a powerful tool in generating hope images. At a presentation of photographs submitted to an "Images of Hope" project and coordinated with music from an "Images of Hope" tape,[6] the audience reported they felt somehow stronger, somehow more hopeful. Many hospitals and care facilities have begun music therapy programs. Research is now confirming the benefits.

Look for hope models

Everyone has someone who can act as a "hope model": a real person, a storybook character, or a television personality. A hope model, not uncommonly, has attributes that the patient needs or admires. By understanding the hope model, patients may be able to take on the role and strengths of the hope model when their own hope fails. It may also be possible for patients to look at the strengths and weaknesses of different coping styles with an objectivity not possible if they were looking only to themselves.

I am reminded of a patient named Jack who was nearing his emotional limit to tolerate chemotherapy. He found his hope model in a youngster, bald as a peanut, who strolled into his room one day. The boy was pushing his intravenous with one hand, protecting the other from bumps, and carrying a broken toy tucked under his arm pit. He innocently approached and, with his big blue eyes unusually gentle for the circumstances, asked of Jack, "Can you fix my toy?" Jack knew at that moment that if this little fellow could handle cancer, so could he. Murray, too, in his story (page 21) of being "lucky" enough to meet a fourteen-year-old boy who "never gave up," speaks of the hope he gained from his inspirational encounter.

Build hope bridges

Hope is experienced in the present, but it is linked to the past and the future. Strengths and wisdom from the past can be used to construct a bridge to the goals of the future. When transformed into images, they also serve as hope images. Everyone has faced difficulty before and won, or they simply would not be here. Many have managed to face considerable hardship by drawing on personal survival skills, but they may not have thought about their illness as a situation that requires similar skills or attitudes. For example, a banker may never have thought of having arthritis as being similar to running a lending institution. Once the banker recognizes that "bankruptcy of the body" is possible, the principles of good money management can be applied to managing the illness: To win, one has to make more deposits than withdrawals. Bringing the skills of financial management to illness is an example of building a "hope bridge." The skills are already there; they just have to be applied in a new situation.

Create hope symbols

A "hope symbol" can be anything that points beyond itself, that suggests a meaning beyond the concrete: an unopened flower, a winter bulb, a flag, a piece of art, a rosary. Symbols are difficult to talk about because they are indeed symbolic! Symbols, by their vary nature, have unique and particular meaning to the person who creates them. A symbol is a personal vehicle for a concept and represents potential for that person and carries that person's emotional attachments. For example, the soldier who carries into battle a picture drawn by his young son is carrying a drawing that has particular meaning and attachment for him; he can use it as a "hope symbol" to help him through a difficult time. For another person, the musical lyrics "Tie a yellow ribbon 'round the old oak tree" may capture the experience of hope. Someone who ties yellow ribbons in the front yard tree is declaring their hope that a loved one will return — from prison, from war, from anything that threatens to break the bond. In this case, the symbol is personal but also has shared meaning with others in the culture. To share something symbolic assumes a common understanding of the symbol. A very familiar example is the case of the greeting card. The greeting card industry is based on the capacity for a card to symbolize caring. How many times have you pondered in a card shop, looking for just the right card? The card is an attempt to convey a relationship, to represent caring. For many of us, a bedside table abounding in Get Well cards serves as a symbolic picture of the caring of people who sent them.

Offer hope suggestions

It is possible in everyday interactions with people to embody hope suggestions by our actions and by our use of language. When the physician gives a patient an appointment three months in the future, the implication is that the patient will be around to keep the appointment. When a professional caregiver says, "I am not sure whether your symptoms will be gone by tomorrow morning or whether it will take a little longer," the suggestion is that the symptoms could be less by the next day. On the other hand, when a pharmacist says, "The drugs don't work for about three days," probably they won't! If the pharmacist says instead, "People vary; the drug will likely be effective within three days; some people experience relief sooner," some people will! The use of language is a powerful instrument of hope. Words can convey possibility or can imply that there are no alternatives.

Share "hopeful" humor

The therapeutic use of humor is now well known. If the patient is a close relative or friend, you will have a sense of the kind of humor they appreciate. If you do not know the patient well, remember that humor is dependent on understanding a good deal about the patient and/or family, even if at an intuitive level. Humor is often culture bound. What is funny in one culture is puzzling or even rude to another. While inappropriate humor is unwelcome, I believe, as visitors and professionals, we could risk more. Send a funny card, bring a book of cartoons instead of chocolates, ask if anything even a little funny has happened during the stay in the hospital.

The therapeutic value of humor is now sufficiently recognized that some hospitals and institutions have "humor rooms" or "humor pro-grams." Laughter apparently releases substances within our bodies that serve as natural pain killers and anti-depressants. Increasingly, I have noticed that physicians are exchanging their pharmaceutical calendars for framed cartoons in their treatment rooms.

Leo was in the last stages of liver cancer. When he came to my office, he looked egg-yoke yellow. He reported that a hoped-for decision was not possible, that his ex-wife was already closing in for part of his estate, that his lawyer had said, "Don't worry, you're basically bankrupt," and that the pain was becoming intolerable. For some reason my spon-taneous response was, "Other than that, how's your week been?" I was immediately concerned I had been inappropriate. However, Leo was laughing so hard I could hardly understand him as he said, "Thank goodness, someone still thinks I am alive! I am so tired of everyone treating everything so seriously."

Look for hope

How do you look for the element of hope in a difficult situation? Here are some questions to guide your thinking:

- What is this person hoping for?
- How committed is this person to that specific hope?
- On what basis is this person adhering to that hope?
- Have I let this person know that I understand what she/he is hoping for?
- To what degree is there the hope that "I" have the answer?
- What hope(s) do I have for this person?
- How do I feel about this person's expectations?
- Have I let this person know the limits of what I can offer?
- Have I offered my "self"? Have I made a "real" connection?
- Have I conveyed empathy, warmth, regard, genuineness?
- Have I suggested alternative targets for their hope?
- Have I suggested an alternative view of the situation?
- Have I a hopeful story, image, or humorous anecdote I can share with this person?

Sustain your own hope

The role of a caregiver — professional or otherwise — can be taxing. Idealism wears thin as the demands of patients, the developments of technology, the policies of governments and institutions, the chronic exposure to suffering, the demands of family and other relationships, and the mixed blessing of aging take their toll. Like the ill people we know or care about, our health and well-being will be influenced by our vision of the future. Having a vision allows us to measure our progress not only by the events of a single day, but also by our contribution to the greater picture. Having a vision is a way of reminding ourselves of the important questions: "Why am I here? What am I really doing? How am I allowing myself to get sidetracked?" Without reflecting on these questions, we are subject to the discouragements of financial difficulties, limited resources, strained relationships. Each of us formulates our own version of meaning that we hope to live out. I cannot know yours. I will, however, close by sharing mine:

I have a dream — a vision of how caring could be. Of how having been ill wouldn't mean fear and loneliness — wouldn't mean long days of anxiety. That it could mean coming to an institution that cared — not just one person caring — not just an individual nurse, a unique doctor, a gentle orderly. Where a whole institution of caring people understood that nothing is as therapeutic as recognizing the emotional pain, not just the physical pain. I have a vision that doctors could talk compassionately. That families could talk openly. That patients could talk freely. That death could be something to be faced, not feared.

I have a vision that the caregivers would touch patients, gently, caringly and not only physically. That all would recognize that with every touch, every smile, every word, we enter a temple. A temple so sacred, so impressionable, so beautiful that every fingerprint leaves its mark. That with every moment we enter the temple of the self.

I have a vision that caregivers would share a strength — a strength that comes only from a common purpose, that comes from belonging to a community of people who believe that caring makes a difference, that custodians matter as much as physicians, that volunteers have a place beside nurses, that letters and titles matter less than kindness.

That line-ups are no more. That people are cared for before paper. That voices convey caring before directions. That waiting rooms reflect hope rather than convenience. That death means knowing a lot of people care. That there will be no physical pain and no aloneness. That tears could give way to laughter and anger to tenderness. That joy could surface in our sadness.[7]

NOTES

[1] Nekolaichuk, 1990.

[2] Menninger, 1959.

[3] Cousins, 1989, p. 2.

[4] Suzuki, 1990.

[5] White and Epston, 1990, p. x.

[6] The "Images of Hope" music tape is composed by Adam Martin Geiger and is available on cassette from LuraMedia.

[7] Adapted from Ronna Jevne's article "I Have a Dream," which appeared in *Humane Medicine*, 1987.

BIBLIOGRAPHY

Cheren, S. (Ed.). (1989). *Psychosomatic Medicine: Theory, Physiology and Practice, Vol.1.* Madison, CT: International University Press, Inc.

Cousins. N. (1989). *Head First: The Biology of Hope.* New York: Dutton.

Day, J. P. (1969). "Hope." *American Philosophical Quarterly, 6* (2), 89–102.

Dufault, K. (1981). "Hope of Elderly Persons with Cancer." Unpublished doctoral dissertation, Case Western Reserve University, Cleveland, Ohio.

Dufrane, K., & Leclair, S. W. (1984). "Using Hope in the Counseling Process." *Counseling and Values, 29*(1), 32–41.

Frank, J. (1968). "The Role of Hope in Psychotherapy." *International Journal of Psychiatry, 5*, 383–395.

French, T. M. (1958). *The Integration of Behavior, Vol. 3: The Reintegration Process in a Psychoanalytic Treatment.* Chicago: Chicago University Press.

Jevne, R. (1987). "I Have a Dream." *Humane Medicine, 3*(2), 147.

Laney, M. L. (1969). "Hope as a Healer." *Nursing Outlook, 13*(1), 45–46.

Manrique, J. F. D. (1984). "Hope as a Means of Therapy in the Work of Karen Horney." *The American Journal of Psychoanalysis, 44*(3), 301–310.

Menninger, K. (1959). "The Academic Lecture on HOPE." *The American Journal of Psychiatry, 116*(12), 481–491.

Miller, J., & Powers, M. J. (1988). "Development of an Instrument to Measure Hope." *Nursing Research, 37*(1), 6–10.

Nekolaichuk, C. (1990). "The Relationship Between Hope, Medication Compliance and Chronic Illness." Unpublished master's thesis, University of Alberta, Edmonton, Alberta.

Orne, M. (1968). "On the Nature of Effective Hope." *International Journal of Psychiatry, 5*, 403–410.

Owen, D. C. (1989). "Nurses' Perspectives on the Meaning of Hope in Patients with Cancer: A Qualitative Study." *Oncology Nursing Forum, 16*(1), 75–79.

Staats, S. (1989). "Hope: A Comparison of Two Self-report Measures for Adults." *Journal of Personality Assessment, 53*(2), 366–375.

Suzuki, D. (1990, August 26). "Scientists Must Allow 'Love' and 'God' into Their Vocabulary." *The Edmonton Journal,* E5.

Wakelee-Lynch, J. (1989). "Hope." *Guideposts, 32*(3), 1,18.

White, M., & Epston, D. (1990). *Narrative Means to Therapeutic Ends.* New York: W. W. Norton.

Yalom, I. (1985). *The Theory and Practice of Group Psychotherapy.* New York: Basic Books.

RONNA FAY JEVNE

About the Author

Ronna Fay Jevne, Ph.D., is a Professor of Counselling in the Department of Educational Psychology
at the University of Alberta. In addition, she is a
member of the Doctorate of Ministry Clinical Di-
vision Committee of St. Stevens Theological Col-
lege, a guest lecturer with the Faculty of Medicine,
and a Research Associate with the Cross Cancer
Institute where she was formerly the Head of the
Department of Psychology. Her involvements
across disciplines reflect her unique background and training in English, Philosophy, Psychology, and Theology. As an active psychologist, researcher,
educator, and consultant, she has a long-standing interest in psychological
issues related to chronic and life-threatening illness. Elske Consulting Associ-
ates, founded by Ronna Jevne and her husband, Allen, responds to educational
and psychological needs of individuals and organizations, including hospitals,
schools, self-help organizations, and government agencies involved with chronic
illness.

As a national and international speaker, Jevne lectures on subjects including managing the stress of illness, dealing with grief and loss, care of the
caregiver, holistic health issues, and her favorite topic, hope. As well as being
co-author with A. Levitan of *No Time for Nonsense: Getting Well Against the
Odds*, Jevne is author of *Managing the Stress of Cancer* and over forty professional articles.

Jevne is a founding member of the Canadian Association of Psychosocial
Oncology, an interdisciplinary organization concerned with the psychosocial
aspects of cancer, and a director of the Canadian Guidance and Counselling
Association. As such she was Program Chair for the 1989 National "Strategies
for Wellness" Conference. For her work in the area of chronic illness, she has
been recognized in *International Who's Who in Medicine* and *Foremost Women
of the Twentieth Century.*

Ronna Jevne shares her life with her husband, Allen, and her stepchildren,
foster sons, and grandchildren. For leisure, she and Allen work on the "hope
projects," a series of projects investigating hope enhancement.

LuraMedia Publications

Marjory Zoet Bankson, BRAIDED STREAMS: Esther and a Woman's Way of Growing
(ISBN 0-931055-05-09)

SEASONS OF FRIENDSHIP: Naomi and Ruth as a Pattern *(ISBN 0-931055-41-5)*

Carolyn Stahl Bohler, PRAYER ON WINGS: A Search for Authentic Prayer
(ISBN 0-931055-72-5)

Alla Renée Bozarth, WOMANPRIEST: A Personal Odyssey *(ISBN 0-931055-51-2)*

Mary Cartledge-Hays, TO LOVE DELILAH: Claiming the Women of the Bible
(ISBN 0-931055-68-7)

Judy Dahl, RIVER OF PROMISE: Two Women's Story of Love and Adoption
(ISBN 0-931055-64-4)

Judith Duerk, CIRCLE OF STONES: Woman's Journey to Herself *(ISBN 0-931055-66-0)*

Lura Jane Geiger and Patricia Backman, BRAIDED STREAMS: Leader's Guide
(ISBN 0-931055-09-1)

Lura Jane Geiger and Susan Tobias, SEASONS OF FRIENDSHIP: Leader's Guide
(ISBN 0-931055-74-1)

Lura Jane Geiger, Sandy Landstedt, Mary Geckeler and Peggie Oury, ASTONISH ME,
YAHWEH!: A Bible Workbook-Journal *(ISBN 0-931055-01-6)*

Kenneth L. Gibble, THE GROACHER FILE: A Satirical Exposé of Detours to Faith
(ISBN 0-931055-55-5)

Ronna Fay Jevne, Ph.D. and Alexander Levitan, M.D., NO TIME FOR NONSENSE:
Self-Help for the Seriously and Chronically Ill *(ISBN 0-931055-63-6)*

Ted Loder, EAVESDROPPING ON THE ECHOES: Voices from the Old Testament
(ISBN 0-931055-42-3 HB; ISBN 0-931055-58-X PB)

GUERRILLAS OF GRACE: Prayers for the Battle *(ISBN 0-931055-04-0)*

NO ONE BUT US: Personal Reflections on Public Sanctuary *(ISBN 0-931055-08-3)*

TRACKS IN THE STRAW: Tales Spun from the Manger *(ISBN 0-931055-06-7)*

Joseph J. Luciani, Ph.D., HEALING YOUR HABITS: Introducing Directed Imagination, a
Successful Technique for Overcoming Addictive Problems *(ISBN 0-931055-71-7)*

Jacqueline McMakin with Sonya Dyer, WORKING FROM THE HEART: For Those Who
Hunger for Meaning and Satisfaction in Their Work *(ISBN 0-931055-65-2)*

Richard C. Meyer, ONE ANOTHERING: Biblical Building Blocks for Small Groups
(0-931055-73-3)

Elizabeth O'Connor, SEARCH FOR SILENCE, Revised Edition *(ISBN 0-931055-07-5)*

Donna Schaper, A BOOK OF COMMON POWER: Narratives Against the Current
(ISBN 0-931055-67-9)

SUPERWOMAN TURNS 40: The Story of One Woman's Intentions to Grow Up
(ISBN 0-931055-57-1)

Renita Weems, JUST A SISTER AWAY: A Womanist Vision of Women's Relationships in
the Bible *(ISBN 0-931055-52-0)*

*LuraMedia is a company that searches for ways to encourage personal growth, shares the excitement
of creative integrity, and believes in the power of faith to change lives.*

7060 Miramar Rd., Suite 104
San Diego, California 92121